PRINCIPLES AND PRACTICES OF MANAGEMENT

A STUDY MATERIAL FOR BTTM

ANN ROSE ANGELS T. M.COM | M.PHIL

Copyright © Ann Rose Angels T. M.com , M.phil
All Rights Reserved.

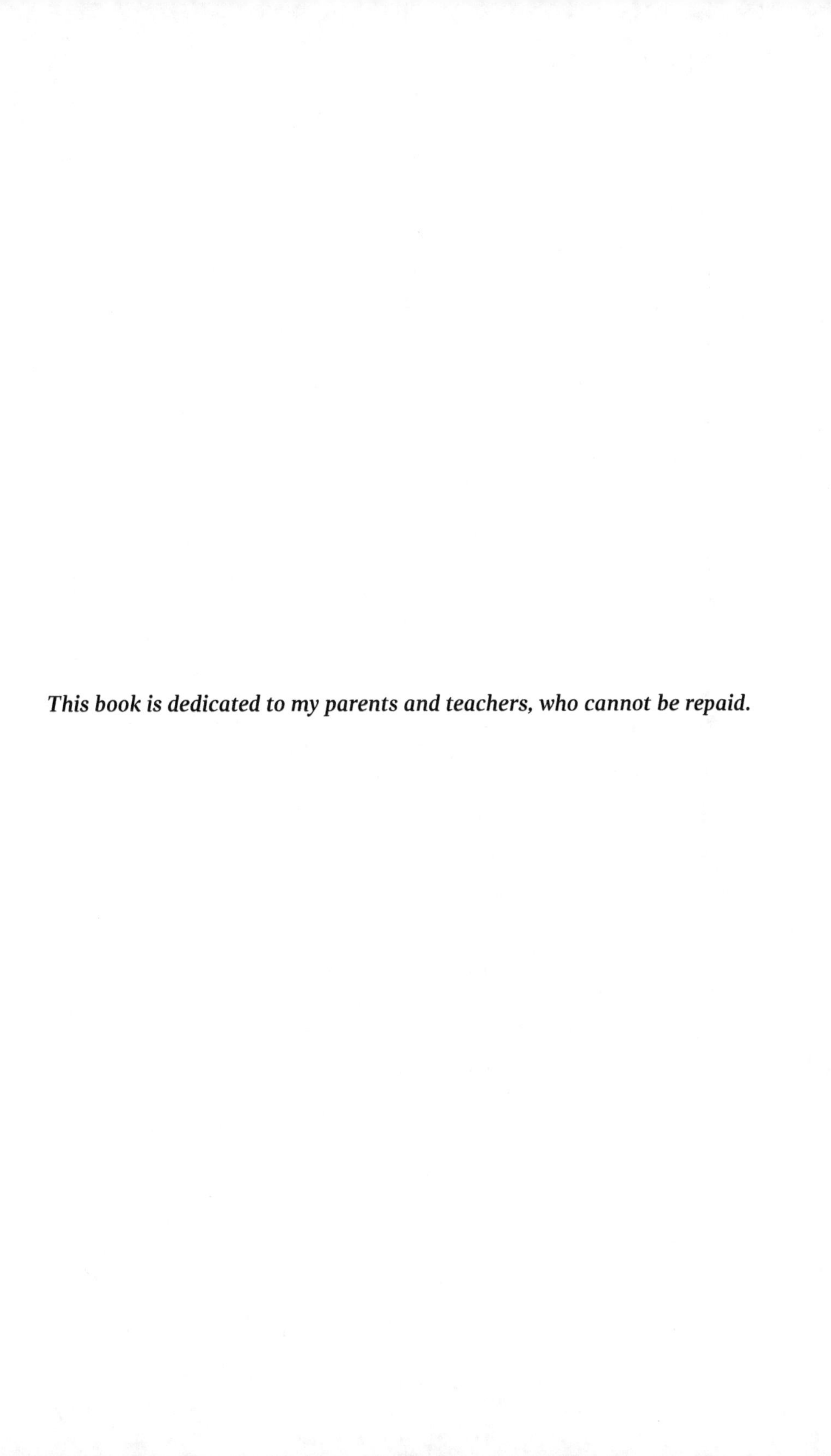

This book is dedicated to my parents and teachers, who cannot be repaid.

Contents

Preface

It gives me great pleasure to present the book Principles and Practices of Management to you. The objective when developing material for each chapter was to provide students with a solid and comprehensive foundation in the fundamentals of management. To acquaint students with the terms, concepts, and points of view used in management. Each of the chapters is comprehensive. The book is written in a direct, active style that hopes students find both readily accessible and immediately relevant. The book follows a student-friendly approach.

Though I have taken great care in avoiding mistakes, if there are still any, I shall feel obliged to those who will point them out.

Ann Rose Angels T

July 2022

CHAPTER I

INTRODUCTION TO MANAGEMENT

Management is the art and science of managing others. A manager's primary challenge is to solve problems creatively, and management often refers to "the art of getting things done through the efforts of other people." The principles of management are the means by which you work to accomplish tasks through others individually, in groups, or in organizations. Formally defined, the principles of management are the activities that "plan, organize, and control the operations of the basic elements of people, materials, machines, methods, money, and markets, providing direction and coordination, and giving leadership to human efforts, so as to achieve the sought objectives of the enterprise."For nearly a century, principles of management have been discussed using the P-O-L-C framework, which refers to the management functions of planning, organizing, leading, and controlling. While managers do not necessarily spend all their time managing, everyone employed in an organization is affected by management principles, processes, policies, and practices. Consequently, finding a "way to do it better" is a challenge that helps all individuals to meet their personal and professional goals.

Who is a Manager?

Managers are the people in the organization responsible for developing and carrying out this management process. A manager is a role represented within a hierarchy of an organization, starting from the CEO and trickling down to the vice president, director, and then finally department managers. The manager is the communication line between an executive team and employees working under them who work together to execute projects and complete their goals

The managerial process can be described as

(1) Anticipating potential problems or opportunities and designing plans to deal with them

(2) Coordinating and allocating the resources needed to implement plans

(3) Guiding personnel through the implementation process, and

(4) Reviewing results and making any necessary changes. This last stage provides information to be used in ongoing planning efforts, and thus the

cycle starts over again.

The four functions are highly interdependent, with managers often performing more than one of them at a time and each of them many times throughout a normal workday.

Types of managers

A large organization can have multiple managers to streamline operations and communication lines. Managers can have different titles that portray their contributions to their department, and their titles make it easier for employees to ask relevant questions too.

The different types of managers that can exist within an organization are:

- Top managers: They're heavily involved in a company's strategy. Everything they oversee must align with the company's mission for it to be successful.
- General managers: They manage the success of a product line or the unit that's producing revenue. They can make choices on what the plan is for a product and create goals for that plan.
- Line managers: Line managers must generate specific output for services a company provides to its customers. Results need to be reported to them so they can communicate them to upper management.
- Team managers or supervisors: Supervisors hold a management role within a subgroup of an organization. They oversee a particular function that requires people to complete and manage before it's reported to upper management. This could consist of a manager reporting to a manager depending on the company's structure.

<u>**Skills for Managers**</u>

Managers need to have a dynamic skill set to thrive within their roles. Some of these skills include:

Management skills

A manager must complete tasks and people, so it can be a delicate balance to work with, but a manager knows when to be supportive and when to hold employees accountable. Their impeccable organization skills give them the time to compartmentalize and focus on the well-being of their team members. They can also create project plans and delegate important responsibilities to trusted employees that can meet their deadlines on specific tasks.

Communication skills

The way a manager communicates to their employees can determine the relationship they have with an employee or a member of the executive team. Managers must be constantly aware of their surroundings and tailor their communication style to the situation they're in. For example, a manager can offer constructive criticism to an employee during a performance review that results in a better performance in the future, or they can listen to the executive team and take effective notes on how to carry out a company's strategic plan.

Customer service skills

A manager needs to be ready to express empathy when working with a customer. The result of an empathetic manager is that a customer can have a long-term relationship with you and employees working alongside you can take note of your behavior and take note when they interact with customers.

Leadership skills

A manager must guide employees to reach their targeted goals. The way a manager leads and acts under different circumstances has a domino effect on the rest of the department. Being a quality leader is going to require risk-taking, time management, and the ability to cultivate a team environment that empowers employees to demonstrate their best performance.

FUNCTIONS AND RESPONSIBILITIES OF MANAGERS

The managers work to increase the efficiency and effectiveness of their employees, processes, projects, and organizations as a whole. Workplaces depend on the strength of those in management positions. In addition to directing employees, managers must communicate with more senior professionals in their company to ensure the team meets the goals and furthers the company's mission. Although the duties of managers differ based on their industry and workplace, must fulfill the same basic responsibilities. The four primary functions of managers are planning, organizing, leading, and controlling.

<u>Functions of manager</u>

The functions of a manager are the various roles played by the manager in an organization. A manager is accountable for all the happenings in the firm and is answerable to the management. The seven major roles played by the manager are –

- **Planning:** The manager needs to plan the schedule and give the blueprint of how the task is to be done with all the necessary details, and also the manager should have a backup plan that if this doesn't work then what next. Example – There is a new project, how to start, human resources required, resources required, etc., everything should be planned.

- **Organizing:** The manager needs to synchronize and have to make sure everything is going according to the plan. Everything should work as per the plan, and if not, then the manager needs to look into the issue and make it work as planned. When assigning team member roles, managers should explain and ensure that employees understand their duties. To help employees feel engaged and productive, managers should ensure that employees are assigned an appropriate amount of work and an appropriate amount of time to complete their work.
- **Staffing:** Staffing means grouping people into different teams and allotting different tasks to them. If the team members have some disputes then the team member needs to report to the team leader who will forward it to the manager and the issue will be taken care of. Example – Assembling a new team for a new project.
- **Directing/leading:** It is a manager's responsibility to guide the employees in all situations to avoid conflicts and delays in the task. The manager has to lead the employees so that they can get a clear idea about what is to be done and how to do it. For example – a team needs a team leader to look after each task that is accomplished, in process, or aborted.
- **Coordinating:** It means bringing all the employees together by forming an efficient relationship and making them feel comfortable to share their views and issues freely. Example – Coordinating the schedule for a project.
- **Reporting:** The manager has to keep updated information about all the ongoing tasks, and it is the sole responsibility of the manager to report the updated status to the higher authorities; while all the employees are bound to report to the manager. Example – Keeping the respective directors informed about the progress of their respective projects.
- **Budgeting:** A task has to be completed within the given time frame as well as it should be cost-efficient. The manager needs to be doubly sure that all the amount invested in the project doesn't exceed the budget given and in case of imbalance, the budgeting manager has to report to the management. Example – If the budget allows placing three employees then five employees cannot be assigned for the task.
- **Controlling:** Controlling is the process of evaluating the execution of the plan and making adjustments to ensure that the organizational goal

is achieved. During the controlling stage, managers perform tasks such as training employees as necessary and managing deadlines. Managers monitor employees and evaluate the quality of their work. They can conduct performance appraisals and give employees feedback, providing positive remarks on what they are doing well and suggestions for improvement.

Responsibilities of manager

- *Acts as the middleman between upper management and their employees:* A manager is accountable for communicating an executive team's goal and announcing the responsibilities of each employee in their department. Managers participate in meetings with the executive team and ask questions in regards to clarity about an organization's goals. They also help brainstorm future goals that benefit the organization's customers and employees. A manager must be attentive and proactive to be successful in this role and to help the employees under them to carry out organizational tasks.
- *Acts as the middleman between customers and the organization:* Managers also serve customers that receive the work presented by the organization, including members of their department. Customers render their feedback on if the quality of the product they receive is up to their standards. Managers also work with their employees to make adjustments based on customer feedback, so they're constantly working with multiple channels to finish complex projects on time.
- *Teaches employees skills to help them complete projects:* A manager is held accountable by the executive team to make sure their employees meet their goals. Managers help employees when they're working on specific tasks and they can be a motivator and a support system for employees during times of adversity. Managers spend most of their time training new employees to help them get acclimated to their new positions with the organization.
- *Hires employees:* A department manager is considered the hiring manager who interviews applicants to see if they're the right fit for the job. Managers prepare questions and examine the answers given by interviewees to see if their answer meets their criteria.
- *Conducts performance reviews:* Managers evaluate the performance of each employee individually. This usually happens on an annual basis, but

this can also occur quarterly or every six months. Managers can suggest ways for employees to improve and achieve larger goals set out by the organization, or they can hear feedback from employees.

- *Makes decisions for department problems:* A manager may encounter a scenario where they have to intervene in a dispute between two or more employees within their department. A manager has the choice to handle it internally with the members of the department or have human resources assist in these cases. Managers normally work with human resources to settle disputes and ensure a quick resolution.

What is management?

The term is derived from the verb which can mean: to organize, to control, to handle, to carry out for a purpose, etc. There are different applications of the term management. It can be used to refer to the following aspects:

An occupational group is a group of people performing managerial tasks and functions. It is used collectively to refer to all the individuals in the group.

An individual who performs managerial functions or is a part of a group involved in the management functions.

An academic discipline, an area of specialisation that imparts knowledge and skills in management

The concept of Management can be defined as the process of achieving things to achieve goals effectively and efficiently. Management is the process of working with people and other organizational resources and reaching organizational goals. Management is the coordination and administration of tasks to achieve a goal. Such administration activities include setting the organization's strategy and coordinating the efforts of staff to accomplish these objectives through the application of available resources. Management can also refer to the seniority structure of staff members within an organization.

Management is the process of guiding the development, maintenance, and allocation of resources to attain organizational goals. Management is dynamic by nature and evolves to meet the needs and constraints in the organization's internal and external environments.

The term 'management' has been used in various senses:

Management can be referred to as the process of planning, organizing, staffing, directing, coordinating, and controlling, at other times it is used to describe people as the task of managing them. It is also known as the body of knowledge, practice, and discipline.

Some people describe the concept of management as a leadership and decision-making technique, while others have analyzed management as a process of economic resources, production factors, or authority.

Definition of management:

"To manage is to forecast and to plan, to organize, to command, to coordinate and to control"- Henry Fool.

"Management is getting things done through the efforts of other people"- Lawrence A Appley

"Management is the art of getting things done through and with people informally organized groups. It is the art of creating an environment in which people can perform as individuals and yet co-operate towards attainment of groups goals"-Harold Koontz

"Management is the planning, organising, command, coordination, and control of the technical, financial security, and accounting activities". -Louis A Alen

In the words of Henry Fayol, "To manage is to forecast and to plan, to organise, to command, to coordinate and to control".

According to Peter F Drucker, "Management is a multi-purpose organ that manages a business and manages managers and manages worker and work".

Nature of Management

An analysis of the various definitions of management indicates that management has certain characteristics. The following are the salient characteristics of management.

1. Management aims at reaping rich results in economic terms: Manager's primary task is to secure productive performance through planning, direction, and control. It is expected of the management to bring into being the desired results. Rational utilisation of available resources to maximise profit is the economic function of a manager. A professional manager can prove his administrative talent only by economising the resources and enhancing profit.

2. Management also implies skill and experience in getting things done through people: Management involves doing the job through people. The economic function of earning a profitable return cannot be performed without enlisting co-operation and securing a positive response from "people". Getting the suitable type of people to execute the operations is a significant aspect of management. In the words of Koontz and O'Donnell, "Management is the art of getting things done through people informally organised groups".

3. Management is a process: Management is a process, function, or activity. This process continues till the objectives set by the administration are actually achieved. "Management is a social process involving coordination of human and material resources through the functions of planning, organising, staffing, leading and controlling in order to accomplish stated objectives".

4. Management is a universal activity: Management is not applicable to business undertakings only. It applies to political, social, religious, and educational institutions also. Management is necessary when group effort is required.

5. Management is a science as well as an art: Management is an art because there are definite principles of management. It is also a science because of the application of these principles predetermined objectives can be achieved.

6. Management is a profession: Management is gradually becoming a profession because there are established principles of management that are being applied in practice, and it involves specialised training and is governed by an ethical code arising out of its social obligations.

7. Management is an endeavour to achieve pre-determined objectives: Management is concerned with directing and controlling the various activities of the organisation to attain the pre-determined objectives. Every managerial activity has certain objectives. In fact, management deals particularly with the actual directing of human efforts.

8. Management is a group activity: Management comes into existence only when there is a group activity towards a common objective. Management is always concerned with group efforts and not individual efforts. To achieve the goals of an organisation management plans, organize, coordinate, directs, and controls the group effort.

9. Management is a system of authority: Authority means power to make others act in a predetermined manner. Management formalises a standard set of rules and procedures to be followed by the subordinates and ensures their compliance with the rules and regulations. Since management is a process of directing men to perform a task, authority to extract the work of others is implied in the very concept of management.

10. Management involves decision-making: Management implies making decisions regarding the organisation and operation of the business in its different dimensions. The success or failure of an organisation can be judged by the quality of decisions taken by the managers. Therefore, decisions are the key to the performance of a manager.

11. Management implies good leadership: A manager must have the ability to lead and get the desired course of action from the subordinates. According to R. C. Davis, "management is the function of executive leadership everywhere". Management of the high order implies the capacity of managers to influence the behaviour of their subordinates.

12. Management is dynamic and not static: The principles of management are dynamic and not static. It has to adapt itself according to social changes.

13. Management draws ideas and concepts from various disciplines: Management is an interdisciplinary study. It draws ideas and concepts from various disciplines like economics, statistics, mathematics, psychology, sociology, anthropology, etc.

PROCESS/ FUNCTIONS OF MANAGEMENT

The management process involves the performance of certain fundamental functions. One useful classification of managerial function has been given by Luther Gulick, who abbreviates them using the word POSDCORB – Planning, Organizing, Staffing, Directing, Co-Ordinating, Reporting, and Budgeting. George R Terry has mentioned four fundamental functions of management, Planning, Organizing, Actuating, and Controlling. But the most widely accepted functions of management given by Koontz O'Donnel i.e. Planning, Organizing, Staffing, Directing, and Controlling. In short, different scholars in the field of management have their own classification of functions of management.

Planning

It is the basic function of management. It deals with chalking out a future course of action & deciding in advance the most appropriate course of action for the achievement of pre-determined goals.

According to Koontz, "Planning is deciding in advance - what to do when to do & how to do. It bridges the gap from where we are & where we want to be". A plan is a future course of action. It is an exercise in problem-solving & decision-making.

Planning is a determination of courses of action to achieve desired goals. Thus, planning is systematic thinking about ways & means for the accomplishment of pre-determined goals. Planning is necessary to ensure the proper utilization of human & non-human resources. It is all-pervasive, it is an intellectual activity and it also helps in avoiding confusion, uncertainties, risks, wastages, etc.

Organizing

It is the process of bringing together physical, financial, and human resources and developing productive relationships amongst them for the achievement of organizational goals.

According to Henry Fayol, "To organize a business is to provide it with everything useful or its functioning i.e. raw material, tools, capital and personnel's". Organize a business involves determining & providing human and non-human resources to the organizational structure. Organizing as a process involves:

*Identification of activities.

*Classification of the grouping of activities.

*Assignment of duties.

*Delegation of authority and creation of responsibility.

*Coordinating authority and responsibility relationships.

Staffing

The main purpose of staffing is to put the right man on the right job. It is the function of manning the organization structure and keeping it manned. Staffing has assumed greater importance in recent years due to advancements in technology, increases in the size of businesses, the complexity of human behavior, etc.

According to Kootz & O'Donnell, "Managerial function of staffing involves manning the organization structure through the proper and effective selection, appraisal & development of personnel to fill the roles designed un the structure".

Staffing involves:

- Manpower Planning (estimating manpower in terms of searching, choosing the person, and giving the right place).
- Recruitment, Selection & Placement.
- Training & Development.

- Promotions & Transfer.
- Performance Appraisal
- Remuneration.

Directing

It is that part of the managerial function which actuates the organizational methods to work efficiently for the achievement of organizational purposes. It is considered the life-spark of the enterprise which sets in motion the action of people because planning, organizing, and staffing are the mere preparations for doing the work.

Direction is that inert-personnel aspect of management that deals directly with influencing, guiding, supervising, and motivating sub-ordinate for the achievement of organizational goals. Direction has the following elements:

*Supervision

*Motivation

*Leadership

*Communication

Supervision- implies overseeing the work of subordinates by their superiors. It is the act of watching & directing work & workers.

Motivation- means inspiring, stimulating, or encouraging the subordinates with zeal to work. Positive, negative, monetary, and non-monetary incentives may be used for this purpose.

Leadership- may be defined as a process by which a manager guides and influences the work of subordinates in the desired direction.

Communication- is the process of passing information, experience, opinion, etc from one person to another. It is a bridge of understanding.

Controlling

It implies measurement of accomplishment against the standards and correction of deviation if any to ensure achievement of organizational goals. The purpose of controlling is to ensure that everything occurs in conformity with the standards. An efficient system of control helps to predict deviations before they actually occur.

According to Theo Haimann, "Controlling is the process of checking whether or not proper progress is being made towards the objectives and goals and acting if necessary, to correct any deviation".

According to Koontz & O'Donell "Controlling is the measurement & correction of performance activities of subordinates in order to make sure that the enterprise objectives and plans desired to obtain them as being accomplished". Therefore controlling has the following steps:

- Establishment of standard performance.
- Measurement of actual performance.
- Comparison of actual performance with the standards and finding out deviation if any.
- Corrective action.

SCOPE OF MANAGEMENT

The field of management is very wide. The operational areas of business management may be classified into the following categories:

(i)Production Management: Production management implies planning, organising, directing, and controlling the production function so as to produce the right goods, in the right quantity, at the right time, and at the right cost.

It includes the following activities:

(a) designing the product

(b) location and layout of plant and building

(c) planning and control of factory operations

(d) operation of purchase and storage of materials

(e) repairs and maintenance

(f) inventory cost and quality control

(g) research and development etc.

(ii)Marketing Management: Marketing management refers to the identification of consumer's needs and supplying them with the goods and services which can satisfy these wants. It involves the following activities:

(a) marketing research to determine the needs and expectations of consumers

(b) planning and developing suitable products

(c) setting appropriate prices

(d) selecting the right channel of distribution, and

(e) promotional activities like advertising and salesmanship to communicate with the customers

(iii) Financial Management: Financial management seeks to ensure the right amount and type of funds for business at the right time and at a reasonable cost. It comprises the following activities:

(a) estimating the volume of funds required for both long-term and short-term needs of the business

(b) selecting the appropriate source of funds

(c) raising the required funds at the right time

(d) ensuring proper utilisation and allocation of raised funds so as to maintain the safety and liquidity of funds and the creditworthiness and profitability of the business, and

(e) administration of earnings

Thus, financial management involves the planning, organising, and controlling of financial resources.

(iv)Personnel Management: Personnel management involves planning, organising, and controlling the procurement, development, compensation, maintenance, and integration of human resources of an organisation. It consists of the following activities:

(a) manpower planning

(b) recruitments,

(c) selection,

(d) training

(e) appraisal,

(f) promotions and transfers,

(g) compensation,

(h) employee welfare services, and

(i) personnel records and research, etc

MANAGEMENT THOUGHTS

The schools of management thought are theoretical frameworks for the study of management. Each of the schools of management thought is based on somewhat different assumptions about human beings and the organizations for which they work. Since the formal study of management began late in the 19th century, the study of management has progressed through several stages as scholars and practitioners working in different eras focused on what they believed to be important aspects of good management practice. Over time, management thinkers have sought ways to organize and classify the voluminous information about management that has been collected and disseminated. These attempts at classification have resulted in the identification of management schools.

Different writers have identified as few as three and as many as twelve. Those discussed below include

(1) the classical school,

(2) the behavioral school,

(3) the quantitative or management science school,

(4) the systems school,

(5) the contingency school.

1. THE CLASSICAL SCHOOL

The classical school is the oldest formal school of management thought. Its roots are in the late 19th century and early 20th century. The Classical school is sometimes called the traditional school of management among practitioners. The classical school of thought generally concerns ways to manage work and organizations more efficiently. Three areas of study that can be grouped under the classical school are scientific management, administrative management, and bureaucratic management.

SCIENTIFIC MANAGEMENT.

In the late 19th century, management decisions were often arbitrary and workers often worked at an intentionally slow pace. There was little in the way of systematic management and workers and management were often in conflict. Scientific management was introduced in an attempt to create a mental revolution in the workplace. It can be defined as the systematic study of work methods to improve efficiency. Frederick W. Taylor was its main proponent. Other major contributors were Frank Gilbreth, Lillian Gilbreth, and Henry Gantt.

Scientific management has several major principles.

First, it calls for the application of the scientific method to work to determine the best method for accomplishing each task.

Second, scientific management suggests that workers should be scientifically selected based on their qualifications and trained to perform their jobs optimally.

Third, scientific management advocates genuine cooperation between workers and management based on mutual self-interest.

Finally, scientific management suggests that management should take complete responsibility for planning the work and that workers' primary responsibility should be implementing management's plans.

Other important characteristics of scientific management include the scientific development of difficult but fair performance standards and the implementation of a pay-for-performance incentive plan based on work standards.

ADMINISTRATIVE MANAGEMENT.

Administrative management focuses on the management process and principles of management. In contrast to scientific management, which deals largely with jobs and works at the individual level of analysis, administrative management provides a more general theory of management. Henri Fayol is the major contributor to this school of management thought.

Fayol was a management practitioner who brought his experience to bear on the subject of management functions and principles. He argued that management was a universal process consisting of functions, which he termed planning, organizing, commanding, coordinating, and controlling. Fayol believed that all managers performed these functions and that the functions distinguished management as a separate discipline of study apart from accounting, finance, and production. Fayol also presented fourteen principles of management, which included maxims related to the division of work, authority and responsibility, unity of command and direction, centralization, subordinate initiative, and team spirit.

BUREAUCRATIC MANAGEMENT.

Bureaucratic management focuses on the ideal form of organization. Max Weber was the major contributor to bureaucratic management. Based on observation, Weber concluded that many early organizations were inefficiently managed, with decisions based on personal relationships and loyalty. He proposed that a form of organization, called a bureaucracy, characterized by division of labor, hierarchy, formalized rules, impersonality, and the selection and promotion of employees based on ability, would lead to more efficient management. Weber also contended that managers' authority in an organization should be based not on tradition or charisma but on the position held by managers in the organizational hierarchy.

Bureaucracy has come to stand for inflexibility and waste, but Weber did not advocate or favor the excesses found in many bureaucratic organizations today. Weber's ideas formed the basis for modern organization theory and are still descriptive of some organizations.

2. THE BEHAVIORAL SCHOOL

The behavioral school of management thought developed, in part, because of perceived weaknesses in the assumptions of the classical school. The classical school emphasized efficiency, process, and principles. Some felt that this emphasis disregarded important aspects of organizational life, particularly as it related to human behavior. Thus, the behavioral school focused on trying to understand the factors that affect human behavior at work.

HUMAN RELATIONS.

The Hawthorne Experiments began in 1924 and continued through the early 1930s. A variety of researchers participated in the studies, including Clair Turner, Fritz J. Roethlisberger, and Elton Mayo, whose respective books on the studies are perhaps the best known.

One of the major conclusions of the Hawthorne studies was that workers' attitudes are associated with productivity.

Another was that the workplace is a social system and informal group influence could exert a powerful effect on individual behavior.

A third was that the style of supervision is an important factor in increasing workers' job satisfaction.

The studies also found that organizations should take steps to assist employees in adjusting to organizational life by fostering collaborative systems between labor and management. Such conclusions sparked increasing interest in the human element at work; today, the Hawthorne studies are generally credited as the impetus for the human relations school.

According to the human relations school, the manager should possess skills for diagnosing the causes of human behavior at work, interpersonal communication, and motivating and leading workers. The focus became satisfying worker needs. If worker needs were satisfied, wisdom held, the workers would in turn be more productive. Thus, the human relations school focuses on issues of communication, leadership, motivation, and group behavior. The individuals who contributed to the school are too numerous to mention, but some of the best-known contributors include Mary Parker Follett, Chester Barnard, Abraham Maslow, Kurt Lewin, Renais Likert, and Keith Davis. The human relations school of thought still influences management theory and practice, as contemporary management focuses much attention on human resource management, organizational behavior, and applied psychology in the workplace.

BEHAVIORAL SCIENCE.

Behavioral science and the study of organizational behavior emerged in the 1950s and 1960s. The behavioral science school was a natural progression of the human relations movement. It focused on applying conceptual and analytical tools to the problem of understanding and predicting behavior in the workplace. However, the study of behavioral science and organizational behavior was also a result of criticism of the human relations approach as simplistic and manipulative in its assumptions about the relationship between worker attitudes and productivity. The study of behavioral science in business schools was given increased credence by the 1959 Gordon and Howell report on higher education, which emphasized the importance to management practitioners of understanding human behavior.

The behavioral science school has contributed to the study of management through its focus on personality, attitudes, values, motivation, group behavior, leadership, communication, and conflict, among other issues. Some of the major contributors to this school include Douglas McGregor, Chris Argyris, Frederick Herzberg, Renais Likert, and Ralph Stogdill, although there are many others.

3. THE QUANTITATIVE SCHOOL

The quantitative school focuses on improving decision-making via the application of quantitative techniques. Its roots can be traced back to scientific management.

MANAGEMENT SCIENCE AND MIS.

Management science (also called operations research) uses mathematical and statistical approaches to solve management problems. It developed during World War II as strategists tried to apply scientific knowledge and methods to the complex problems of war. The industry began to apply management science after the war. George Dantzig developed linear programming, an algebraic method to determine the optimal allocation of scarce resources. Other tools used in the industry include inventory control theory, goal programming, queuing models, and simulation. The advent of the computer made many management science tools and concepts more practical for industry. Increasingly, management science and management information systems (MIS) are intertwined. MIS focuses on providing needed information to managers in a useful format and at the proper time. Decision support systems (DSS) attempt to integrate decision models, data, and the decision-maker into a system that supports better management decisions.

PRODUCTION AND OPERATIONS MANAGEMENT.

This school focuses on the operation and control of the production process that transforms resources into finished goods and services. It has its roots in scientific management but became an identifiable area of management study after World War II. It uses many of the tools of management science.

Operations management emphasizes the productivity and quality of both manufacturing and service organizations. W. Edwards Deming exerted a tremendous influence in shaping modern ideas about improving productivity and quality. Major areas of study within operations management include capacity planning, facilities location, facilities layout, materials requirement planning, scheduling, purchasing, and inventory control, quality control, computer integrated manufacturing, just-in-time inventory systems, and flexible manufacturing systems.

4. SYSTEMS SCHOOL

The systems school focuses on understanding the organization as an open system that transforms inputs into outputs. This school is based on the work of a biologist, Ludwig von Bertalanffy, who believed that a general systems model could be used to unite science. Early contributors to this school included Kenneth Boulding, Richard Johnson, Fremont Kast, and James Rosenzweig.

The systems school began to have a strong impact on management thought in the 1960s as a way of thinking about managing techniques that would allow managers to relate different specialties and parts of the company to one another, as well as to external environmental factors. The systems school focuses on the organization as a whole, its interaction with the environment, and its need to achieve equilibrium. General systems theory received a great deal of attention in the 1960s, but its influence on management thought has diminished somewhat. It has been criticized as too abstract and too complex. However, many of the ideas inherent in the systems school formed the basis for the contingency school of management.

5. CONTINGENCY SCHOOL

The contingency school focuses on applying management principles and processes as dictated by the unique characteristics of each situation. It emphasizes that there is no one best way to manage and that it depends on various situational factors, such as the external environment, technology, organizational characteristics, characteristics of the manager, and characteristics of the subordinates. Contingency theorists often implicitly or explicitly criticize the classical school for its emphasis on the universality of management principles; however, most classical writers recognized the need to consider aspects of the situation when applying management principles.

The contingency school originated in the 1960s. It has been applied primarily to management issues such as organizational design, job design, motivation, and leadership style. A few of the major contributors to this school of management thought include Joan Woodward, Paul Lawrence, Jay Lorsch, and Fred Fiedler, among many others.

Principles of management

Fayol's principles of management

Henry Fayol, also known as the 'father of modern management theory' gave a new perception of the concept of management. He introduced a general theory that can be applied to all levels of management and every department. The Fayol theory is practiced by managers to organize and regulate the internal activities of an organization. He concentrated on accomplishing managerial efficiency.

The fourteen principles of management created by Henri Fayol are explained below.

1. Division of Work-

Dividing the full work of the organization among individuals and creating departments is called the division of work. This leads to specialization, and specialization helps to increase efficiency and efficiency which results in improvements in the productivity and profitability of the organization. This principle is appropriate for both the managerial as well as technical work levels. Fayol believed that segregating work in the workforce amongst the worker will enhance the quality of the product. Similarly, he also concluded that the division of work improves the productivity, efficiency, accuracy, and speed of the workers.

2. Authority and Responsibility-

These are the two key aspects of management. Authority facilitates the management to work efficiently, and responsibility makes them responsible for the work done under their guidance or leadership. According to Henri Fayol, there should be a balance between Authority (Power) and Responsibility (Duties). The right to give orders should not be considered without reference to responsibility. If the authority is more than responsibility then chances are that a manager may misuse it. If responsibility is more than authority then he may feel frustrated.

3. Discipline-

Discipline means respect for the rules and regulations of the organization. Discipline may be Self-discipline, or it may be Enforced discipline. The workers must respect the rules that run the organization. To establish discipline, good supervision and impartial judgment are needed.

Without discipline, nothing can be accomplished. It is the core value of any project or any management. Good performance and sensible interrelation make the management job easy and comprehensive. Employee's good behaviour also helps them smoothly build and progress in their professional careers.

4. Unity of Command-

According to this principle, a subordinate (employee) must have and receive orders from only one superior (boss or manager). This means an employee should have only one boss and follow his command. If an employee has to follow more than one boss, there begins a conflict of interest and can create confusion.

5. Unity of Direction-

Unity of direction means activities aimed at the same objective should be organized so that there are one plan and one person in charge. Whoever is engaged in the same activity should have a unified goal. This means all the people working in a company should have one goal and motive which will make the work easier and achieve the set goal easily.

6. Subordination of Individual Interest-

The interest of one individual or one group should not prevail over the general good. The individual interest should be given less importance, while the general interest should be given the most importance. This indicates a company should work unitedly towards the interest of a company rather than personal interest. Be subordinate to the purposes of an organization. This refers to the whole chain of command in a company.

7. Remuneration-

Remuneration is the price for services received. Pay should be fair to both the employee and the firm. This plays an important role in motivating the workers of a company. Remuneration can be monetary or non-monetary. However, it should be according to an individual's efforts they have made. Compensation should be based on a systematic attempt to reward good performance.

8. Centralization and decentralisation -

It is always present to a greater or lesser extent, depending on the size of the company and the quality of its managers. In centralization, the authority is concentrated only in a few hands. In decentralization, the authority is distributed to all the levels of management. No organization can be completely centralized or decentralized. There should be a balance between centralization and decentralization.

The degree to which centralization or decentralization should be adopted depends on the specific organization, but managers should retain final responsibility but should give subordinates enough authority to do the tasks successfully.

9. Scalar Chain-

The chain of command, sometimes called the scalar chain, is the formal line of authority, communication, and responsibility within an organization. Fayol on this principle highlights that the hierarchy steps should be from the top to the lowest. This is necessary so that every employee knows their immediate senior also they should be able to contact any if needed.

10. Order

This principle says that there should be a material and social order in an organisation. The arrangement of things is called material order. the arrangement of people is called social order. A company should maintain a well-defined work order to have a favorable work culture. A positive atmosphere in the workplace will boost positive productivity. There should be a place for everyone and everything in an organisation. The right man should be appointed to the right job.

11. Equity-

Equity is a combination of kindness and justice. It creates loyalty and devotion in the employees toward the organization. The equity principle suggests that the managers must be kind as well as equally fair to the subordinates. All employees should be treated equally and respectfully. It's the responsibility of a manager that no employees face discrimination.

12. Stability of Tenure of Personnel-

Fayol says that employees need to be given fair enough time to settle into their jobs. An employee needs time to learn his job and to become efficient. An employee delivers the best if they feel secure in their job. It is the duty of the management to offer job security to their employees.

13. Initiative-

The management should support and encourage the employees to take initiatives in an organization. It will help them to increase their interest and make them worth it. Management should encourage the employees to make their own plans and to execute these plans.

14. Esprit de Corps-

Esprit de Corps means "Team Spirit". Therefore, the management should create unity, co-operation, and team-spirit among the employees. It is the responsibility of the management to motivate their employees and be supportive of each other regularly. Developing trust and mutual understanding will lead to a positive outcome and work environment.

These 14 principles of management are used to manage an organization and are beneficial for prediction, planning, decision-making, organization and process management, control, and coordination. They work as a guideline for managers to do their job according to their responsibility.

CHAPTER II

PLANNING

An organization can be successful in effective utilization of its human, financial and material resources only when its management decides in advance its objectives and methods of achieving them. Planning involves the determination of objectives of the business, formation of programs and courses of action for their attainment, development of schedules and timings of action, and assignment of responsibilities for their implementation. Planning is the most crucial and foremost function of management. It is defined as the process of setting goals and choosing the means to achieve those goals. Sound planning is imperative for the successful achievement of the goals in the desired direction. It is rightly said, "well plan is half done". It involves setting objectives and goals, designing appropriate strategy and courses of action, and framing plans and procedures, etc for the execution of the proposed activities under the project.

DEFINITIONS

According to George R Terry, "Planning is the selecting and relating of facts and making and using of assumptions regarding the future in the visualization and formulation of proposed activities believed necessary to achieve desired results."

According to Henry Fayol, "Planning is deciding the best alternatives among others to perform different managerial operations in order to achieve the predetermined goals." Generally speaking, planning is deciding in advance what is to be done, that is, a plan is a projected course of action.

CHARACTERISTICS

1. Planning is looking into the future.

2. Planning involves a pre-determined line of action.

3. Planning discovers the best alternative out of available many alternatives.

4. Planning requires considerable time for implementation.

5. Planning is a continuous process.

6. Planning's object is to achieve pre-determined objectives in a better way.

7. Planning integrates various activities of organisation.

8. Planning is done for a specific period.

9. Planning not only selects the objectives, but also develops policies, programs, and procedures to achieve the objectives.

10. Planning is required at all levels of management.

11. Planning is an inter-dependent process that coordinates various business activities.

12. Planning directs the members of the organisation.

13. Growth and prosperity of any organisation depend upon planning.

NATURE OF PLANNING

- Planning is goal-oriented: Every plan must contribute in some positive way towards the accomplishment of group objectives. Planning has no meaning without being related to goals.
- The primacy of Planning: Planning is the first of the managerial functions. It precedes all other management functions.
- The pervasiveness of Planning: Planning is found at all levels of management. Top management looks after strategic planning.
- Middle management is in charge of administrative planning. Lower management has to concentrate on operational planning.
- Efficiency, Economy, and Accuracy: The efficiency of the plan is measured by its contribution to the objectives as economically as possible. Planning also focuses on accurate forecasts.
- Co-ordination: Planning coordinates the what, who, how, where, and why of planning. Without coordination of all activities, we cannot have united efforts.
- Limiting Factors: A planner must recognize the limiting factors (money, manpower, etc) and formulate plans in light of these critical factors.
- Flexibility: The process of planning should be adaptable to changing environmental conditions.
- Planning is an intellectual process: The quality of planning will vary according to the quality of the mind of the manager.

PURPOSE OF PLANNING

- To manage by objectives: All the activities of an organization are designed to achieve certain specified objectives. However, planning makes the objectives more concrete by focusing attention on them.

- To offset uncertainty and change: The future is always full of uncertainties and changes. Planning foresees the future and makes the necessary provisions for it.
- To secure economy in operation: Planning involves, the selection of the most profitable course of action that would lead to the best result at the minimum costs.
- To help in coordination: Co-ordination is, indeed, the essence of management, the planning is the base of it. Without planning it is not possible to coordinate the different activities of an organization.
- To make control effective: The controlling function of management relates to the comparison of the planned performance with the actual performance. In the absence of plans, management will have no standards for controlling other's performance.
- To increase organizational effectiveness: Mere efficiency in the organization is not important; it should also lead to productivity and effectiveness. Planning enables the manager to measure the organizational effectiveness in the context of the stated objectives and take further actions in this direction.

OBJECTIVES OF PLANNING

1. Reduces uncertainty – Future is an uncertainty. Planning may convert uncertainty into certainty. This is possible to some extent by, planning which is necessary to reduce uncertainty.

2. Brings co-operation and coordination – Planning can bring co-operation and coordination among various sections of the organisation. The rivalries and conflicts among departments could be avoided through planning. Besides, planning avoids duplication of work.

3. Economical in operation – Planning selects the best alternatives among various available alternatives. This will lead to the best utilisation of resources. The objectives of the organisation are achieved easily.

4. Anticipates unpredictable contingencies – Some events could not be predicted. These events are termed contingencies. These events may affect the smooth functioning of an enterprise. The planning provides a provision to meet such contingencies and tackle them successfully.

5. Achieving the pre-determined goals – Planning activities are aimed at achieving the objectives of the enterprise. The timely achievements of objectives are possible only through effective planning.

6. Reduce competition – The existence of competition enables the enterprise to get a chance for growth. At the same time, stiff competition should be avoided. It is possible, to reduce competition through planning.

ADVANTAGES OF PLANNING

Planning is one of the crucial functions of management. It is basic to all other functions of management. There will not be proper organization and direction without proper planning. It states the goals and means of achieving them

(i) Planning helps management to face the future with greater strength and confidence.

(ii) It helps to focus attention on the objectives.

(iii) It leads the operational life of the enterprise along the most efficient lines.

(iv) It enables the exercise of control.

(v) It acts as a spur to creativity and innovation.

(vi) It guides the decision-making process.

(vii) It provides a sense of direction for action.

(viii) It facilitates coordination.

(ix) It fosters inter-departmental co-operation.

LIMITATIONS OF PLANNING

Following are the limitations of Planning

1. Time-consuming: The management cannot prepare any plan without taking much time. A number of steps are required to complete the planning process.

2. Costly: It is considered an expensive process. A lot of money is to be spent on the collection, analysis, and editing of data.

3. False sense of security: The management people think that there is security if planning properly adheres. But this is not true in practice.

4. Technological changes: The management is not in a position to change its policies according to technological changes. It will affect the planning process.

5. Political climate: A change in the political climate leads to a change in the policy and attitude towards different financial aspects. It will affect the planning process.

6. Lack of reliable data: The success of all the plans is based on the availability of reliable data. It is very difficult to procure reliable data.

7. Initiative: Planning compels everyone to work as per plan. It reduces the scope for initiation on the part of employees and they will become more

mechanical.

8. Limitations of forecasts: Planning is fully based on forecasts. If there is any defect in forecasts, the planning will lose its value.

TYPES OF PLANNING

1. CORPORATE PLANNING AND FUNCTIONAL PLANNING:

Planning activity is pervasive and can be undertaken at various levels of an organization. It may be for the organization as a whole or its different functions. Thus, based on the coverage of activities, there may be planning for the organization as a whole, known as corporate planning, or for its different functions, known as functional planning.

i. Corporate Planning:

Corporate planning is undertaken at the top level, also known as the corporate level, and covers the entire organizational activities. It is integrative and integrates the entire planning process of the organization. The basic focus of corporate planning is to determine the long-term objectives of the organization as a whole and to generate plans to achieve these objectives bearing in mind the probable changes in the environment. Corporate planning, generally, has a long-term orientation and provides the basis for functional planning.

ii. Functional Planning:

Functional planning is segmental and is undertaken for each major function of the organization like production/operations, marketing, finance, human resource, etc. At the second level, functional planning is undertaken for sub-functions within each major function.

A basic feature of functional planning is that it is derived out of corporate planning and, therefore, it should contribute to the latter. This contribution is achieved by integrating and coordinating functional planning with corporate planning.

2. STRATEGIC PLANNING AND OPERATIONAL PLANNING:

Based on the importance of content, planning may be divided into:
Strategic planning and operational planning.

i. Strategic Planning:

Strategic plans are all about, why things need to happen. Strategic planning includes a high-level overview of the entire business. It's the foundational basis of the organization and will dictate long-term decisions. Strategic planning involves setting the organization's long-term direction in which it wants to proceed in the future. It is the process of deciding the organization's long-term objectives and defining where the organizational resources and efforts should be put to achieve organizational objectives.

Strategic planning deals with strategic issues like the type of business to be undertaken, diversification of business into new lines, type of products to be offered, and so on. This way, strategic planning encompasses all the functional areas of business and is affected within the existing and long-term framework of environmental factors. Strategic planning also involves rigorous analysis of various environmental factors to relate the organization relates to its environment.

ii. Operational Planning:

Operational plans are about how things need to happen. This type of planning typically describes the day-to-day running of the company. Operational planning, also known as tactical planning, is the process of deciding the most effective use of the resources already allocated through strategic planning and developing a control mechanism to ensure effective implementation of the actions so that organizational objectives are achieved.

Usually, operational planning covers one year or so. It aims at sustaining the organization in its production/generation and distribution of current products (goods and services) to the existing markets.

Operational planning answers the questions about a particular action as follows:

a. Why is the action required?
b. What action is to be taken?
c. What will the action accomplish?
d. What are the likely results of the action?
e. What conditions must be met in putting the action in operation?

Operational planning is undertaken within the framework of strategic planning. Examples of operational planning are adjusting production within a given capacity, increasing the efficiency of operating activities through analysis of past performance, budgeting future costs, specific details of future short-term operations, etc.

Difference between Strategic Planning and Operational Planning:

Apart from the period involved in strategic planning and operational planning, there are certain differences between the two.

i. Range of Choice:

Strategic planning guides the choice among the broad directions in which the organization seeks to move and allocate its financial, physical, and human resources over a future specified period. On the other hand, operational planning focuses on the ways and means in which each of the individual functions may be programmed so that progress may be made towards the attainment of organizational objectives.

ii. Type of Environment:

The type of environment for the two types of planning is different. Strategic planning takes into account the external environment and tries to relate the organization with it. The nature of the external environment, thus, is of prime concern to strategic planners. Operational planning mostly focuses on the internal organizational environment to make effective use of given resources.

iii. Focus

Strategic planning focuses on setting long-term trends and direction for managerial actions. Operational planning focuses on making effective use of organizational resources allocated by the strategic planning process.

iv. Sequence of Formulation:

Strategic planning precedes operational planning and the latter is primarily concerned with the implementation of the former. Therefore, operational planning is based on strategic planning.

v. Level of Formulation:

Strategic planning is formulated by top-level management with the support of specified planning staff in the organization. At this level, managers can take an overall view of the organization and can relate the organization with its environment. Operational planning is usually spread over a wide range within the organization and is generally performed by operating managers with the help of the subordinate staff.

3. LONG-TERM PLANNING AND SHORT-TERM PLANNING:

Planning is concerned with the future course of action. This may be long-term or short-term. Thus, there are long-term planning and short-term planning.

i. *Long-term Planning:*

Long-term planning is strategic and involves more than one year period, usually 3-5 years, though a period of 5 years is more common in the Indian context. Long-term planning usually covers all the functional areas of the business and is undertaken within the existing and the long-term future environmental scenario. In the long-term planning process, high emphasis is placed on the analysis of environmental factors.

Sometimes, basic changes in the organization like change in organizational vision and mission, the major change in organizational structure, change in key personnel of the organization, etc. Become a significant factor for long-term planning.

ii. Short-term Planning:

Short-term planning usually covers one year. This aims at making effective use of organizational resources — financial, physical, and human resources. Short-term planning directly and immediately affects functional areas — production, marketing, finance, etc.

Coordination of Short-Term Planning and Long-Term Planning:

In fact, in a successful planning process, short-term plans are made about long-term plans because short-term plans contribute to long-term plans. As such, there is a need for coordination between these two plans. While preparing the short-term plans, the managers should consider that they Eire contributing to the long-term plans.

For this purpose, they should scrutinize the former in the light of the latter. People at comparatively lower levels should also be made aware of this fact. Sometimes, the short-term plans do not contribute to long-term plans, though they may contribute to achieving immediate organizational objectives, for example, cutting the cost of research and development to show higher profitability. This type of problem may be overcome by coordination in short-term planning and long-term planning.

Planning Process

It is not necessary that a particular planning process is applicable for all organization and for all types of plans because the various factors that go into the planning process may differ from plan to plan or from one organization to another.

Perception of Opportunities:- It is the beginning of the planning process. This provides an opportunity to set the objectives in a real sense. It helps to take the advantage of opportunities and avoid threats. Once the opportunities are perceived, the other steps of planning are undertaken.

1. Establishing the objectives:- This stage deals with the setting of major organisational and unit objectives. The organizational objectives should be specified in all key areas. Once organizational objectives are identified, objectives of lower units can be identified in that context.

2. Establishing planning premises:- It means deciding the condition under which planning activities will be undertaken. Planning premises may be external or internal. The nature of planning premises differs at different

levels of planning.

3. Identification of alternatives:- This point says that particular objectives can be achieved through various actions. Since all alternatives cannot be considered for further analysis, it is necessary for the planner to reduce the number of alternatives.

4. Evaluation of alternatives: - Various alternatives which are considered feasible may be taken for detailed evaluation. It is evaluated on the basis of the contribution of each alternative towards the organizational objectives in the light of its resources and constraints.

5. Selection of alternatives: - After the evaluation, the fittest one is selected. At the same time, a planner must be ready with alternatives, normally known as contingency plans, which can be implemented in a changed situation.

6. Developing supporting plans: - After formulating the basic plan, various plans are devised to support the main plan. These plans are known as derivative plans.

7. Establishing activities: sequence of - After formulating basic and derivative plans, the sequence of activities is determined, so that plans are put into action.

8. Devising a mechanism of Project Monitoring and Evaluation.

Planning Process

Types of Plans

A manager is required to develop several plans to achieve the organizational objectives. Three major types of plans can help managers to achieve their organizational goals.

1. Operational Plans 2. Tactical Plans 3. Strategic Plans

1. Operational Plans: It is one that a manager uses to accomplish his or her job responsibilities. In other words, it is the plan used to achieve operational goals. Operational goals are the specific result expected from the departments, workgroups, and individuals. Operational plans may be single-use plans or ongoing plans.

a. Single-use plans: It is applied to those activities which do not recur or repeat. A special sales program is an example of a single-use plan, because, it deals with the who, what, where, how and how much of an activity. It includes:

(i)Budget: It is a statement of expected results expressed in quantitative terms for a definite period. It is prepared to keep in view the objectives, resources, and of the enterprise. It is a useful control device and helpful in co-coordinating activities. It predicts sources and amounts of income and how much they are used for a specific project.

(ii)Programme: It is a sequence of activities to be undertaken for implementing the policies and achieving the objectives of an organization. It tells what is to be done to achieve the goals.

b. Continuing or ongoing plans: These are usually made once and retain their value over years while undergoing periodic revision and updates. The following plans are included in this category.

(i)Policy: It provides broad guidelines for managers to follow when dealing with important areas of decision-making. It is a general statement that explains how a manager should attempt to handle routine management responsibilities. They are standing answers to recurring questions.

(ii)Procedures: A procedure is a set of step-by-step directions that explains how activities or tasks are to be carried out. An established procedure ensures uniformity of action. Most organization has procedures for purchasing supplies and equipment. By defining steps to be taken and the order in which they are to be done, procedures provide a standardized way of responding to a repetitive problem.

(iii) Rules: It is an explicit statement that tells an employee, what he or she can and cannot do. Rules are definite and rigid. Rules are "do" and "don't" statements put into place to promote the safety of employees and the uniform treatment and behavior of employees. For eg. Rules about absenteeism permit supervisors to make discipline decisions rapidly and with a high degree of fairness.

2. Tactical Plans: These are plans which usually span one year or less. It is concerned with what the lower-level units within each division must do, how they must do it, and who is in charge at each level. Tactics are the means needed to activate a strategy and make it work.

3. Strategic Plan: It is an outline of steps designed with the goals of the entire organization in mind, rather than with the goals of specific divisions. It looks ahead over the four, five, or even more years to move the organization from where it is currently to where it wants to be. The top management strategic plan for the entire organization becomes the framework and sets dimensions for the lower-level planning.

Contingency Plan: These plans are used when the original plan proves inadequate because of changing circumstances.

OBJECTIVES

Meaning of Objectives:

Objectives are the ends for the achievement of which managerial activities are directed. Effective management is possible only through the setting up of objectives and all managerial efforts should be directed to achieve these objectives. Objectives constitute the purpose, the attainment of which is necessary for the business. An organization can grow in an orderly way if well-defined goals have been set. Objectives are a prerequisite for planning. No planning is possible without setting up objectives.

Objectives are not only helpful in planning but also in other managerial functions like organizing, directing, and controlling. Clear-cut objectives help in proper decision-making and in achieving better results. The objectives of the organization should be supported by sub-objectives. The objectives have a hierarchy and a network. The organizations and managers may have multiple goals and at times they may be incompatible and may lead to conflicts within the organization and within the groups too.

Personal interests may have to be subordinated to organizational goals. The words objectives and goals are generally used interchangeably and various authors and practitioners have not made any distinction between the two, so these words will be used for the same meaning here.

Mc. Farland defines objectives, "Objectives are the goals, aims, or purposes that organizations wish to achieve over varying periods of time."

In the words of Terry, "A managerial objective is the intended goal which prescribes definite scope and suggests a direction to efforts of a manager."

Mc. Farland suggests that objectives are the goals that an organization wants to achieve whereas Terry describes objectives as the parameters within which an organization has to work and make efforts to achieve them.

Features of Objectives:

1. Every organization has objectives rather it is started to achieve certain objectives. All the members of an organization channel their energies to achieve the stated goals.

2. The objectives of a business organization may be broad as well as specific. These may be set for the whole organization or different segments of it. The objectives may be for the long term or short periods. The overall objectives of the organization are supported by the sub-objectives. For example, the objective of earning a certain percentage of profit in a particular year will be achievable only if the objectives of the manufacturing, marketing, and finance departments support it.

3. Objectives have a hierarchy. At the organizational level, broad objectives are fixed by the top-level management. The broad objectives are specified at the departmental level and then they are derived for different sections. Various objectives at different levels try to achieve organizational objectives.

4. An organization tries to fulfill the needs and aspirations of society. The organizational objectives should have social sanctions since these are social units. The aspirations of society should be reflected in the business objectives.

5. Business objectives may change as per the environmental changes or changes in social needs. The present objectives may have to be changed as per the new situations. The objective of earning profits has of late been associated with the social responsibility of business. Similarly, new objectives may be added or old objectives may be modified or changed.

6. All organizational objectives are interrelated. The achievement of main objectives will require the achievement of subordinate objectives also. The non-achievement of small objectives will also mean the non-achievement of the main objective. So all the objectives are interrelated and they cannot be taken up independently.

7. Another important characteristic of objectives is their multiplicity. There may be several objectives for which the concern may strive to achieve at the same time. The major objectives may also be more. At every hierarchical level too, the objectives may be many. Different areas of business have their objectives. Management should try to achieve all the objectives efficiently and effectively.

8. The objectives should be based on practical situations. They should also take into account the philosophy and thinking of the management. The objectives should be realistic so that they may be converted into actual performance. Unrealistic objectives do more harm than good because they discourage the employees rather than encourage them.

Classification of Objectives:

Management objectives can be classified as follows:

1. Primary Objectives:

These are the objectives for which a company has been started. Every business aims to earn more and more profits out of its work. Primary objectives are related to the company and not to individuals. Earning profits out of providing goods and services to the customers is the primary objective of a company. The goods and services are provided as per the requirements of customers. Earning profits through customer satisfaction helps in earning goodwill and regular clientele. The production of goods and services as per determined targets will be achieved through the individual goals of employees in the organization.

2. Secondary Objectives:

These objectives help in achieving primary objectives. The targets are identified and efforts are made to increase efficiency and economy in the performance of work. The goals dealing with analysis, advice, and interpretation provide support to goals directed by primary objectives. Secondary objectives, like primary objectives, are impersonal. The primary goal of earning profits through providing goods and services will be achieved if there is a plan to add new products to the market at regular intervals. The goal of adding new products will be a secondary goal which will help in achieving the primary objective.

3. Individual Objectives:

These are the goals that individual members in an organization trying to achieve on a daily, weekly, monthly, or yearly basis. These objectives are achievable as subordinate to primary and secondary goals. Most of the individual objects are economic, psychological, or non-financial rewards that an individual tries to achieve by using resources of time, skill, and effort. An individual tries to satisfy his needs and desires by working in an organization. To motivate individuals for raising their performance, organizations offer varied incentives.

4. Social Objectives:

These are the goals of an organization toward society. These include the obligations required by the community, government agencies, etc. These also include goals intended to further the social, physical, and cultural improvement of society. Social obligations of business have become essential these days. The business has to produce goods and services by taking into consideration the health requirements of people. There are expectations that businesses should also spend a part of their profits for the welfare of the community.

Hierarchy of Objectives:

Objectives form a hierarchy ranging from the broad aim to specific individual objectives. At the top of it, the main goals of the organization are set. The organization has to see its responsibilities towards society and then towards herself. The organization is required to contribute to the welfare of society by providing good quality products at a reasonable cost. The main purpose of the business is to provide a specific level of services or a proper type of goods. The overall objectives of the organization are specified by the top-level management.

The objectives of the key areas are also determined by the higher-level management. The next in hierarchy comes to the objectives of divisions and departments and units and these are decided by middle-level management comprising the Vice-president or functional managers. The objectives of individuals are decided at the bottom of the hierarchy. The junior-level management sets performance standards for individuals.

The hierarchy of objectives is shown in the diagram:

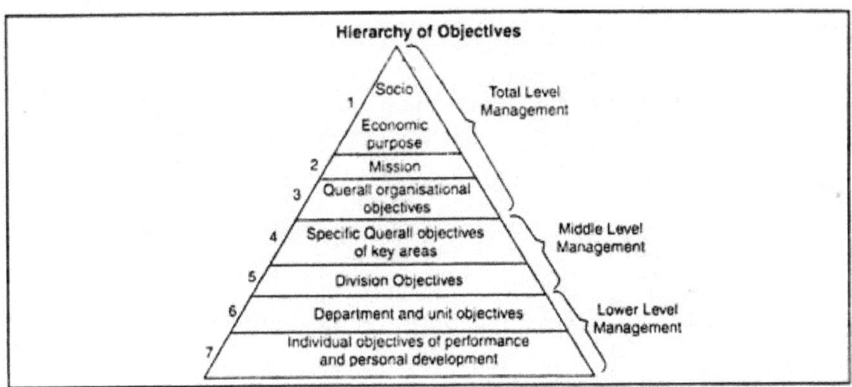

Top-Down and Bottom-up Approach:
There is some controversy about whether the objectives should be fixed top-down or bottom-up. In the top-down approach, upper-level managers

set objectives for the subordinates while in the bottom-up approach subordinates initiate the setting of objectives for their positions and present them to their superiors. The proponents of the top-down approach are of the view that the overall objectives of the organization should be set at the Chief Executive Officer level of the top level of management. It will provide proper synchronization of objectives of different areas and individuals.

On the other hand, the supporters of the bottom-up approach argue that top management needs to have information from lower levels in the form of objectives. Since subordinates fix their own goals they will be motivated and committed to their performance. It may not be advisable to rely entirely on one approach. Both approaches should be used wisely for better results. In a practical situation, such decisions are linked to factors such as the size of the organization, the organization's culture, the leadership style of the executive, and the urgency of the plan.

MANAGEMENT BY OBJECTIVES (MBO)

MBO is both a philosophy and approach to management. It is a process whereby superiors and subordinates jointly identify the common objectives, set the results that should be achieved by the subordinates, assess the contribution of each individual, and integrate individuals with the organization to make the best use of organizational resources. Thus MBO is a system for integrating managerial activities.

According to Koontz and O' Donnel, "MBO is a comprehensive managerial system that integrates many key managerial activities in a systematic manner, consciously directed towards the effective and efficient achievement of organizational objectives"

Features of MBO

The following are the important features of MBO

1. MBO is an approach and philosophy to management and not merely a technique

2. MBO emphasizes objectives.

3. MBO is concerned with the participation of concerned managers in objective setting and performance reviews.

4. MBO reviews performance periodically.

5. Objectives in MBO provide guidelines for appropriate systems and procedures.

6. MBO establishes a community of interest and a shared sense of vision among all the managers.

Process of MBO

The following are the stages involved in the MBO process

1. Setting of organizational objectives

The first step in MBO is the definition of organizational objectives and purpose. Usually, the objective setting starts at the top level of the organization and moves downward to the lowest managerial levels. The setting objective includes defining the purpose of the organization, long-range and short-range organizational objectives, divisional or departmental objectives, and individual manager's objectives.

2. Identification of Key Result Areas

Organizational objectives provide the basis for the identification of Key Result Areas (KRAs). KRAs are derived from the expectations of various stakeholders and they indicate the priorities for organizational performance such as profitability, market standing, innovation, productivity, social responsibility, etc.

3. Setting subordinates' objectives

The achievement of organizational goals is only possible through individuals. So each manager must know in advance what he is expected to attain. Every manager in the managerial hierarchy is both superior and subordinate (except the managers at the top and bottom levels). The process of objective setting begins with the superior's proposed recommendations for his subordinate's objectives. In turn, the subordinates state their objectives as perceived by him. Thereafter the final objectives for the subordinates are set by the mutual negotiation between superiors and subordinates.

4. Matching resources with objectives

Resource availability is an important aspect of objective setting because it is the proper application of resources that ensures objective achievement. So there should be a match between objectives and resources.

5. Appraisal

Appraisal tries to measure whether a subordinate is achieving his objective or not. The appraisal is undertaken as an ongoing process to find out the deficiency in the working and also to remove it promptly to attain the objectives of the organization.

6. Recycling

Though appraisal is the last aspect of the MBO process, it is used as an input for recycling objectives and other actions. The recycling process includes the setting of objectives at various levels, action planning based on those objectives, and performance review. Each of these three aspects gives a base for others. This process goes on continuously.

Benefits of MBO

The benefits of MBO can be seen as follows

1. MBO helps in better managing the orgaisational resources and activities.

2. Since organizational objectives are defined very clearly in MBO, they help in relating the organization to its environment.

3. MBO provides the greatest opportunity for personnel satisfaction because they participated in objective setting and rational performance appraisal.

4. MBO stimulates organizational change and provides a framework and guidelines for organizational change.

Problems and Limitations of MBO

Each organization is likely to encounter specific problems in MBO practice but some of the common problems are as follows

1. MBO is a time-consuming and costly process

2. Manager's failure to teach MBO philosophy

3. Problems in objective setting

4. more emphasis on short-term objectives

5. Danger of inflexibility in the organization in a dynamic environment

6. MBO creates frustration among managers Despite the obstacles and problems in MBO, it continues to be a way of managing an organization.

CHAPTER III

STRATEGIES AND POLICIES

Today, most business enterprises engage in strategic planning, of course, the degree and sophistication vary. Strategic planning analyses the current and expected future situation determines the direction of the firm and develops means for achieving the mission.

The word 'strategy' has entered the field of management from the military where it refers to applying the forces against an enemy to win a war. Originally, the word strategy has been derived from the Greek 'strategos' which means generalship. The word was used the first time around 400 BC. The word strategy means the art of the general fighting in a war. The dictionary meaning of strategy is, "the art of so moving or disposing of the instrument of warfare to impose upon the enemy, the place time and conditions for fighting with oneself." In management, the concept of strategy is taken in broader terms.

According to Glueck, "Strategy is the unified, comprehensive and integrated plan that relates the strategic advantage of the firm to the challenges of the environment and is designed to ensure that the basic objective of the enterprise is achieved through the proper implementation process."

Strategic management is the art and science of formulating, implementing, and evaluating cross-functional decisions that will enable an organization to achieve its objectives. It is the process of specifying the organization's objectives, developing policies and plans to achieve these objectives, and allocating resources to implement the policies and plans to achieve the organization's objectives. Strategic management, therefore, combines the activities of the various functional areas of a business to achieve organizational objectives. It is the highest level of managerial activity, usually formulated by the Board of Directors and performed by the organization's Chief Executive Officer (CEO) and executive team. Strategic management provides overall direction to the enterprise and is closely related to the field of Organization Studies.

Policies are general statements or understandings that guide managers' thinking in decision-making. They ensure that decisions fall within certain boundaries. They usually do not require action but are intended to guide

41

managers in their commitment to the decision they ultimately make.

The essence of the policy is discretion. Strategy, on the other hand, concerns the direction in which human and material resources will be applied to increase the chance of achieving selected objectives.

NATURE OF STRATEGY

A few aspects regarding the nature of the strategy are as follows:

- Strategy is a major course of action through which an organization relates itself to its environment, particularly the external factors to facilitate all actions involved in meeting the objective of the organization.
- Strategy is the blend of internal and external factors. To meet the opportunities and threats provided by the external factors, internal factors are matched with them.
- Strategy is the combination of actions aimed to meet a particular condition, solve certain problems, or achieve a desirable end. The actions are different for different situations.
- Due to its dependence on environmental variables, the strategy may involve a contradictory action. An organization may take contradictory actions either simultaneously or with a gap of time. For example, a firm is engaged in closing down some of its business and at the same time expanding some.
- Strategy is future-oriented. Strategy actions are required for new situations which have not arisen before.
- Strategy requires some systems and norms for its efficient adoption in any organization.
- The strategy provides an overall framework for guiding enterprise thinking and action.

The purpose of strategy is to determine and communicate a picture of the enterprise through a system of major objectives and policies. Strategy is concerned with a unified direction and efficient allocation of an organization's resources. A well-made strategy guides managerial action and thought. It provides an integrated approach for the organization and aids in meeting the challenges posed by the environment.

IMPORTANCE OF STRATEGY

The strategy provides various benefits to its users:

- The strategy helps an organization take decisions on long-range forecasts.
- It allows the firm to deal with a new trend and effectively meet competition.
- With the help of strategy, the management becomes flexible to meet unanticipated future changes.
- Efficient strategy formation and implementation result in financial benefits to the organization in the form of increased profits.
- The strategy provides focus in terms of organizational objectives and thus provides clarity of direction for achieving the objectives.
- Organizational effectiveness is ensured with the effective implementation of the strategy.
- Strategy contributes toward organizational effectiveness by providing satisfaction to the personnel.
- It gets managers into the habit of thinking and thus makes them, proactive and more conscious of their environments.
- It motivates employees as it paves the way for them to shape their work in the context of shared corporate goals and ultimately they work for the achievement of these goals.
- Strategy formulation & implementation allows the management to involve different levels of management in the process.
- It improves corporate communication, coordination, and allocation of resources.

ESSENCE OF STRATEGY
Strategy is characterized by four important aspects.

1. Long-term objectives
2. Competitive Advantage
3. Vector
4. Synergy

LONG TERM OBJECTIVES: Strategy is formulated keeping in mind the long-term objectives of the organization. It is so because it emphasizes long-term growth and development. Strategy is future-oriented and therefore concerned with the objectives which have a long-term perspective. The objectives give directions for implementing a strategy.

COMPETITIVE ADVANTAGE: Whenever a strategy is formulated, managers have to keep in mind the competitors of the organization. The environment has to be continuously monitored for forming a strategy. The strategy has to be made in the sense that the firm may have a competitive advantage. It makes the organization competent enough to meet the external threats and profit from the environmental opportunities. The changes that take place over some time in the environment have made the use of strategy more beneficial. While making plans, competitors may be ignored, but in making, strategy competitors are given due importance.

VECTOR: Strategy involves the adoption of the course of action and allocation of resources for meeting the long-term objectives. From among the various courses of action available, the managers have to choose the one which utilizes the resources of the organization in the best possible manner and helps in the achievement of the organizational objectives. A series of decisions are taken and they are in the same direction.

The strategy provides direction to the whole organization. When the objective has been set, they bring about clarity to the whole organization. They provide clear direction to persons in the organization who are responsible for implementing the various courses of action. Most people perform better if they know clearly what they are expected to do and where the organization is going.

SYNERGY: Once we take a series of decisions to accomplish the objectives in the same direction there will be synergy. Strategies boost the prospects by providing synergy.

MAJOR KINDS OF STRATEGIES AND POLICIES

For a business enterprise (and with some modification. for other kinds of organizations as well,) the major strategies and policies that give an overall direction to operations are likely to be in the following areas

Growth:

Growth strategies give answers to such questions as:

How much growth should occur?

How fast Where?

How should it occur?

Finance:

Every business enterprise and for that matter, any non-business enterprise strategy for financing its operations There are various ways of doing this and usually must have a clear many serious

Organization:

The organizational strategy has to do with the type of organizational pattern an enterprise will use It answers practical questions. For example, how centralized or decentralized should the decision-making authority be? What kinds of departmental patterns are most suitable? How should staff positions be designed? Naturally, organization structures furnish the system of roles and role relationships that help people accomplish objectives

Personnel:

There can be many major strategies in the area of human resources and relationships. They deal with such topics as union relations, compensation selection, hiring, training, and appraisal, as well as with special areas such as job enrichment

Public Relations:

Strategies in this area can hardly be independent, they must support other major strategies and efforts They must also be designed in the light of the company's type of business, its closeness to the public, and its susceptibility to regulation by the Government agencies In any area, strategies can be developed only if the night questions are asked White no set of strategies can be formulated that will fit all organizations and situations, certain key questions will help any company discover what its strategies should be The right questions will lead to answers, For example, some key questions are presented as follows for two major strategic areas products or services and marketing With a little thought you can devise key questions for other major strategic areas

Products or Services:

A business exists to furnish products or services In a very real sense, profits are merely a measure-although important one-of how well a company serves its customers. New products or services, more than any other single factor determining what an enterprise is or will be.

The key questions in this area can be summarized as follows :

- What is our business?
- Who are our customers?
- What do our customers want?
- How much will our customers buy and at what price?
- Do we wish to be product leaders?
- Do we wish to develop our new products?
- What advantages do we have in serving customer needs?
- How should we respond to the existing and potential competition?

- How far can we go in serving customer needs? What profits can we expect?
- What basic form should our strategy take?

Marketing:

Marketing strategies are designed to guide managers in getting products or services to customers and in encouraging customers to buy Marketing strategies are closely related to product strategies, they must be interrelated and mutually supportive As a matter of fact. Peter Drucker regards the two basic business functions as innovation (eg, the creation of new goods or services) and marketing A business can scarcely survive without at least one of these functions and ideally both.

The key questions that serve as guides for establishing a marketing strategy are

- Where are our customers and why do they buy?
- How do our customers buy?
- How is it best for us to sell?
- Do we have something to offer that competitors do not?
- Do we wish to take legal steps to discourage competition?
- Do we need, and can we supply, supporting services?
- What is the best pricing strategy and policy for our operation?

Types of strategies

A strategy is an action plan that sets the direction that a company will be taking. A strategy is a decision-making choice and would involve consideration of the external environment affecting the company as well as the internal environment of strengths and weaknesses of the company. According to William F. Guelick, there are four strategies: stability, growth, retrenchment, or a combination approach.

1. Stability strategy: Stability strategy implies, 'to leave them well enough alone. If the environment is stable and the organization is doing well, then it is better to make no changes. An example of a stability strategy would be an organization that would be satisfied with the same product, serve the same consumer groups, and maintains the same market share.

2. Growth strategy: Growth means expansion of the operations of the company and the addition of new areas of operations. A growth strategy can be very risky and involves forecasting and analysis of many factors that affect expansion, like resource availability and market availability. However, growth is necessary due to the volatility of businesses and industries. Diversification of services or products is another example of growth and strategy. A classic example of the growth of existing services is that of McDonald's Hamburger chain. Starting from scratch in the 1950s, it developed into a franchise chain of 6000 outlets in 1979 with a sale of over US$ 5 billion per year.

3. Retrenchment strategy: Retrenchment primarily means a reduction in products, services, and personnel. This strategy is useful in the face of tough competition, scarcity of resources, and re-organization of the company to reduce waste. Most airlines have streamlined their operations.

4. Combination strategy: Combination strategy means using a combination of other strategies and is primarily used by large complex organizations that may want to cut back in some areas and expand in others. Also, in times of financial difficulties, a company may employ a retrenchment strategy and resort to a growth strategy, if the economic situation improves.

Successful Implementation of Strategies

If strategic planning is to be successful, certain steps must be taken to implement it. Following are the eight recommendations that should be considered by managers who wish to put their strategies to work.

Communicating Strategies to all Key Decision-Making Managers -The priority is to communicate strategies to all those managers who are in a position to make decisions on programs and plans designed to implement them. It is not enough if strategies are clear to the executive committee members and the chief executive who participated in developing them. What is required is that strategies should be communicated in writing. Top executives, and their subordinates, must make sure that everyone involved in implementing strategies understands them.

Developing and Communicating Planning Premises- Planning premises refer to broad assumptions about the environment in which plans will operate. Managers must develop premises critical to plans and decisions, explain them to all those in the decision-making chain, and give instructions to develop programs and make decisions in line with them. Very few organizations do this. But if premises do not include key assumptions about the environment in which plans will operate, decisions are likely to be based on personal assumptions and predilections. This will almost certainly lead to a collection of uncoordinated plans.

Ensuring that Action Plans Contribute to and Reflect Major Objectives and Strategies -Action plans are tactical or operational programs and decisions, major or minor, that take place in various parts of an organization. If they do not reflect the desired objectives and strategies, the result will be vague hopes or useless intentions. If care is not taken in this area, strategic planning is not likely to have a bottom-line impact, that is, they have will not the desired effect on company profits.

There are various ways of making sure that action plans contribute to major goals. If every manager understands strategies, all managers can certainly review the recommendations of staff advisers and line subordinates to see that they contribute and are consistent. It might even be a good idea for major decisions to be reviewed by an appropriate small committee, such as one including a manager's superior, the superior's superior, and a staff specialist. Budgets should also be reviewed with objectives and strategies in mind.

Reviewing StrategiesRegularly- Even carefully developed strategies may cease to be suitable if conditions change. Therefore, they should be reviewed from time to time, certainly not less than once a year for major strategies and perhaps more often.

Developing Contingency Strategies and Program- If a considerable change in competitive factors or other elements in the environment may occur, strategies for such contingencies should be formulated. The future is uncertain and there should be a standby plan and strategy to gear up for any eventuality.

Making the Organization Structure fit Planning Needs -The organization structure, with its system of delegations, should be designed to help the manager accomplish goals and make the decisions necessary to put plans into effect. If possible, one person should be responsible for the accomplishment of each goal and for the implementation of strategies to achieve this goal. Where such an arrangement is not possible, another alternative is to make use of the form of a matrix organization . If this is done, however, the responsibilities of the various positions in the matrix should be clearly defined.

Continuing to Emphasize Planning and Implementing Strategy- Even if an organization has a functional system of objectives and strategies and their implementation, the system can easily fail unless responsible managers continue to stress the nature and importance of these elements. This process may seem tedious and unnecessarily repetitious, but it is the best way to make sure that members of an organization learn about them. Teaching does not necessarily mean conducting seminars; rather, much of the teaching can take place in the day-to-day interaction between superiors and subordinates.

Creating a Company Climate That Forces Planning- People tend to allow problems and crises of today to interfere with effective planning for tomorrow. The only way to ensure that planning will be done is to develop strategies carefully and to take pains to implement them

Importance of Strategy

Strategic management is needed in every organization and it offers several benefits.

1. Universal: Strategy refers to a complex web of thoughts, ideas, insights, experiences, goals, expertise, memories, perceptions, and expectations that provides general guidance for specific actions in pursuit of particular ends. Nations have, in the management of their national policies, found it necessary to evolve strategies that adjust and correlate political, economic, technological, and psychological factors, along with military elements. Be it management of national policies, international relations, or even of a game on the playfield, it provides us with the preferred path that we should take for the journey that we make.

2. Keeping pace with changing environment The present-day environment is so dynamic and fast-changing thus making it very difficult for any modern business enterprise to operate. Because of uncertainties, threats, and constraints, the business corporation is under great pressure and is trying to find out the ways and means for their healthy survival. Under such circumstances, the only last resort is to make the best use of strategic management, which can help the corporate management to explore possible opportunities and at the same time achieve an optimum level of efficiency by minimizing the expected threats.

3. Minimizes competitive disadvantage: It minimizes competitive disadvantage and adds up to competitive advantage. For example, a

company like Hindustan Lever Ltd. realized that merely by merging with companies like Lakme, Milk food, Ponds, Brooke bond, Lipton, etc which makes fast-moving consumer goods alone will not make it market leader but venturing into retailing will help it reap heavy profits. Then emerged its retail giant "Margin Free' which was the market leader in states like Kerala.

4. Clear sense of strategic vision and a sharper focus on goals and objectives: Every firm competing in an industry has a strategy because strategy refers to how a given objective will be achieved. 'Strategy' defines what it is we want to achieve and charts our course in the marketplace; it is the basis for the establishment of a business firm, and it is a basic requirement for a firm to survive and sustain itself in today's changing environment by providing vision and encouraging to define the mission.

5. Motivating employees One should note that labour efficiency and loyalty towards management can be expected only in an organization that operates under strategic management. Every guidance as to what to do, when and how to do it, by whom, etc. is given to every employee. This makes them more confident and free to perform their tasks without any hesitation. Labor efficiency and loyalty which results in industrial peace and good returns are the results of broad-based policies adopted by the strategic management

6. Strengthening Decision-Making: Under strategic management, the first step to be taken is to identify the objectives of the business concern. Hence a corporation organized under the basic principles of strategic management will find smooth sailing due to effective decision-making. This points out the need for strategic management.

7. Efficient and effective way of implementing actions for results: Strategy provides a clear understanding of purpose, objectives, and standards of performance to employees at all levels and in all functional areas. Thereby it makes implementation very smoothly allowing for maximum harmony and synchrony. As a result, the expected results are obtained more efficiently and economically.

8. Improved understanding of internal and external environments of business: Strategy formulation requires continuous observation and understanding of environmental variables and classifying them as opportunities and threats. It also involves knowing whether the threats are serious or casual and whether opportunities are worthy or marginal. As such strategy provides for a better understanding of the environment.

LEVELS OF STRATEGY

It is believed that strategic decision-making is the responsibility of top management. However, it is considered useful to distinguish between the levels of operation of the strategy. The strategy operates at different levels:

- Corporate Level
- Business Level
- Functional Level

There are two categories of companies- one, which has different businesses organized in different directions or product groups known as profit centers or strategic business units (SBUs), and the other, which consists of companies that are single-product companies. The example of the first category can be that of Reliance Industries Limited which is a highly integrated company producing textiles, yarn, and a variety of petrochemical products and the example of the second category could be Ashok Leyland Limited which is engaged in the manufacturing and selling of heavy commercial vehicles. The SBU concept was introduced by General Electric Company (GEC) of the USA to manage product business. The fundamental concept in the SBU is the identification of discrete independent product/ market segments served by the organization. Because of the different environments served by each product, an SBU is created for each independent product/ segment. Every SBU is different from another SBU due to the distinct business areas (DBAs) it is serving. Each SBU has a clearly defined product/market segment and strategy. It develops its strategy, according to its capabilities and needs with the overall organization's capabilities and needs. Each SBU allocates resources according to its requirements for the achievement of organizational objectives. As against the multi-product organizations, the single product organizations have a single Strategic Business unit. In these organizations, corporate-level strategy serves the whole business. The strategy is implanted at the next lower level by functional strategies. In multiple product companies, a strategy is formulated for each SBU (known as business level, strategy) and such strategies lie between corporate and functional level strategies.

The three levels are explained below.

CORPORATE LEVEL STRATEGY

This is among the most important types of strategy formulation as it's used to outline the precise requirement of an organization—growth, acquisition, stability, or retrenchment. This in turn shapes the nature of the work that an organization does, the timeline it has to follow, and the resources that are at its disposal.

At the corporate level, strategies are formulated according to organization-wise policies. These are value-oriented, conceptual, and less concrete than decisions at the other two levels. These are characterized by greater risk, cost, and profit potential as well as flexibility. Mostly, corporate-level strategies are futuristic, innovative, and pervasive. They occupy the highest level of strategic decision-making and cover the actions dealing with the objectives of the organization. Such decisions are made by the top management of the firm. Examples of such strategies include acquisition decisions, diversification, structural redesigning, etc. The board of Directors and the Chief Executive Officer are the primary groups involved in this level of strategy making. In small and family-owned businesses, the entrepreneur is both the general manager and chief strategic manager.

BUSINESS LEVEL STRATEGY

As one of the levels of strategy formulation that requires the most research and investment of time and personnel, the business level strategy has a specific purpose. That purpose is to answer the question—how exactly is an organization going to compete? This takes into account an organization's abilities to expand and retain a competitive edge in the market. This type of strategy formulation is particularly useful for those organizations that have several small units of business, each one of which is considered to be a strategic business unit (SBU).

The strategies formulated by each SBU to make the best use of its resources given the environment, it faces, come under the gamut of business-level strategies. At such a level, strategy is a comprehensive plan providing objectives for SBUs, allocation of resources among functional areas, and coordination between them for the achievement of corporate-level objectives. These strategies operate within the overall organizational strategies i.e. within the broad constraints and policies and long-term objectives set by the corporate strategy. The SBU managers are involved in this level of strategy. The strategies are related to a unit within the organization. The SBU operates within the defined scope of operations by the corporate level strategy and is limited by the assignment of resources at the corporate level. However, corporate strategy is not the total of the business strategies of the organization. Business strategy relates to the "how" and the corporate strategy relates to the "what". Business strategy defines the choice of product or service and market of individual businesses within the firm. The corporate strategy has an impact on business strategy.

FUNCTIONAL LEVEL STRATEGY

This level of strategy is concerned less with ideation and more with logistical management and execution. The focus of this level is primarily on the growth and how daily actions, including allocation of resources, can help deliver corporate and business level strategies for the organization to reach its business goals.

This strategy relates to a single functional operation and the activities involved therein. This level is at the operating end of the organization. The decisions at this level within the organization are described as tactical. The strategies are concerned with how different functions of the enterprise like marketing, finance, manufacturing, etc. contribute to the strategy of other levels. Functional strategy deals with a relatively restricted plan providing objectives for a specific function, allocation of resources among different operations within the functional area, and coordination between them for the achievement of SBU and corporate level objectives.

Sometimes the fourth level of strategy also exists. This level is known as the **operating level**. It comes below the functional level strategy and involves actions relating to various sub-functions of the major function. For example, the functional level strategy of the marketing function is divided into operating levels, such as marketing research, sales promotion, etc.

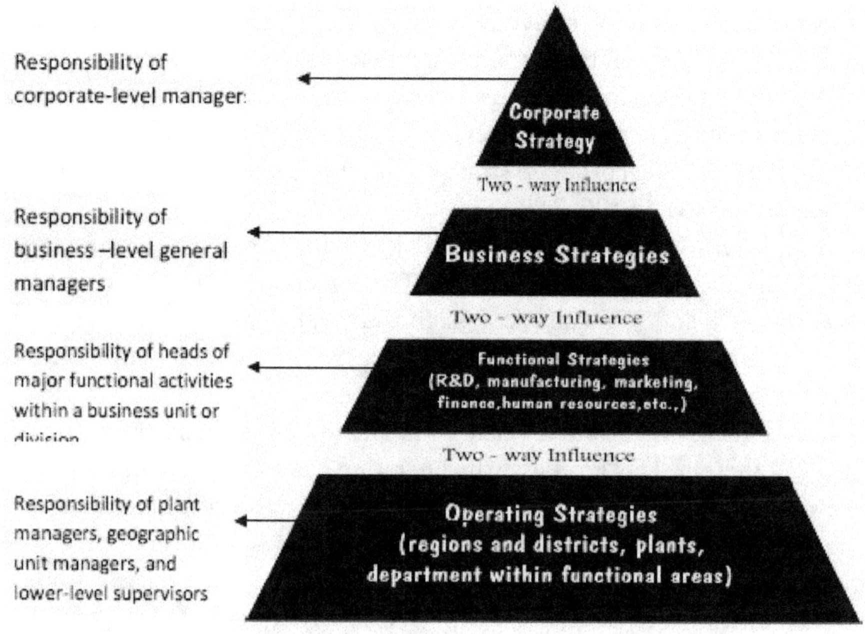

Hierarchy of strategy

FORMULATION OF STRATEGY

Strategy formulation is the process of using available knowledge to document the intended direction of a business and the action steps to reach its goals. This process is used for resource allocation, prioritization, organization-wide alignment, and validation of business goals. it is the process of selecting the most appropriate and efficient ways to realize an organization's vision and help it realize its goals and objectives. The process is a part of strategic management and involves using several analytical tools to figure out the best way to use an organization's resources. Strategy formulation allows an organization to create a financial blueprint for creating profits and being sustainable in the long haul.

The most popular way of examining a strategy formulation process is through the SWOT analysis. SWOT is an acronym for strengths, weaknesses, opportunities, and threats. It provides a detailed and comprehensive analysis of strategy formulation and helps an organization determine whether a particular strategy is fit to be implemented.

STEPS OF STRATEGY FORMULATION

Six separate steps are recognized as part of the strategy formulation process. Each of these steps of strategy formulation has a specific role to play, although it's not mandatory for the steps to follow a specific chronology to be effective. Let's take a closer look at all the steps of strategy formulation with a brief explanation for each.

1. DETERMINING ORGANIZATIONAL OBJECTIVES

The primary purpose of the strategy formulation is to set down certain objectives that an organization tries to meet. Objectives may be ambitious or modest, but in either case, they must be spelled out with the help of a detailed plan that shows how these objectives can be realized by the organization. When determining organizational objectives, strategy formulation also takes care of the periods when particular objectives have to be met or discarded, in case they're no longer feasible within the scope of the industry concerned.

2. ASSESSING THE ORGANIZATIONAL ENVIRONMENT

The second step of strategy formulation involves assessing the industrial and economic environment in which an organization operates. This means that competitors within an industry need to be observed, tracked, and analyzed. In addition to that, regular qualitative and quantitative reviews of an organization's product or services must be carried out.

3. FIXING QUANTITATIVE TARGETS

This step requires organizations to fix quantitative targets that they must meet in a particular quarter or financial year. These targets provide useful information about the long-term value of customers to an organization as well as the performance trajectories of various product or service zones and operating departments across an organization.

4. DIVISIONAL PLANS AND CONTRIBUTIONS FROM DIFFERENT DEPARTMENTS

For this step, each department or division or product, or service category present in an organization is identified and evaluated for its performance and adherence to strategic planning. This is done not only for the department in question but also for each of the sub-units under a single department.

5. PERFORMANCE ANALYSIS

As part of this step, organizations are required to identify and analyze the gap between desired performance and actual performance. This is done based on performance data, customer feedback, employee suggestions as well as a general survey of the trends and patterns present in an organization. This step is vital to building connections between what an organization has done in the past, how it's faring in the present, and what it can accomplish in the future.

6. CHOICE OF STRATEGY

The previous five steps of strategy formulation are supposed to culminate in the sixth and final step of deciding the actual strategy for an organization. To pick the best course of action, this step requires active and careful consideration of organizational strengths and weaknesses, potential, limitations as well as the presence of internal and external opportunities for that organization.

POLICIES

According to Koontz & O Donnel, "Policies were identified as guides to thinking in decision-making. They assume that when decisions are made, these will fall within certain boundaries." Policies do not require action but are intended to guide managers in their decision commitments when they do not make decisions.

In the words of George Terry, "Policy is a verbal, written or implied overall guide setting up boundaries that supply the general limits and direction in which managerial action will take place." Policies provide a framework within which a person has the freedom to act.

Features of a Policy

(i) A policy is a standard plan which provides answers to recurring problems of a similar nature. It provides answers/guidelines to the members of an organization for deciding the future course of action. A policy provides and explains what a member should do rather than what he is doing.

(ii) A policy limits an area within which a decision is to be taken for the achievement of organizational goals. It avoids repeated analysis of situations and allows delegation of powers and still retains control over actions.

(iii) Policies are models of thought and principles underlying the activities of an organization. They guide the behaviour and decisions of the executive.

(iv) Policies are framed by all managers in the organization. There is a need for giving guidelines for future courses of action at every level of management. However, the importance of policy differs according to the level of management. At a higher level of management important policies are decided while at the lower level some less important or minor policies are required.

Purpose of Policies

Policies are regarded as important for realizing the objectives of the organization. They also ensure the coordination of efforts and activities in the enterprise.

The policies are formulated for the following purposes:

1. The main purpose of policies is to ensure that there is no deviation from the planned course of action. The framework is set within which everybody is expected to work. Policies ensure that the broad guides for action are adhered to.

2. Since policies chalk out a framework for every person, it ensures proper delegation of authority also. A manager knows the extent of authority required by a subordinate to undertake the work allotted to him. Policies serve the purpose of delegating adequate authority downwards.

3. Policies allow the scope for interpretation. The main aspects are given in a policy but the actual mode of implementation is decided by the concerned person.

4. Policies are helpful for future planning also. The impact and influence of policies help in thinking about the future.

5. Policies also ensure consistency of action. The guidelines are similar for everybody and actions must conform to the broad outlines.

Aspects should be taken into consideration while framing policies:

1. Organizational Goals: The policies are formed to achieve organizational goals. The goals are the targets that are to be achieved and policies devise ways of reaching them. Policies should assist by basing them on relevant facts and figures and not on mere guesswork.

2. Proper Participation: Policies should be framed by the participation of persons at various levels of management. If policies are framed at top levels without knowing the views of those for whom these are meant then there is a likelihood that policies may not achieve the desired results. To ensure the

successful implementation of policies, there is a need for joint participation at the time of formulating them.

3. Reflect Business Environment: The policies should be based on the internal and external environment. The situation prevailing inside and outside will provide a realistic base for policies. The policies should have the flexibility for adjustment if there is a change in a business environment. Any type of rigidity followed in policies will defeat their purpose.

4. Consistency: Various policies of an enterprise should conform to each other. There should be no inconsistency among various policies. If there is inconsistency among policies, then these will not be implemented. It must be ensured that policies are related to enterprise objectives and do not give conflicting guidelines.

5. Proper Communication: The policies should be properly communicated to each level of management. If the policies are not properly known by those who are to implement them, then there will be no use for such policies. Sometimes policies may not be well understood, there may be some doubt in the minds of people, it will be the duty of management to clarify them and provide proper clarification.

6. In Writing: The policies should always be in writing. This will ensure their proper and correct implementation. If the policies are not in writing, then a dispute may arise about their contents and purpose. The language of policies should also be simple so that it is well understood by concerned persons.

Characteristics of a sound policy

1. A policy should be clearly prescribed and understandable by all. It should be subject to one interpretation and the intent and the content of the policy must be clearly expressed and preferably in writing.

2. It should be stable but sufficiently flexible. Stability implies that no changes in the policy are to be made except in response to fundamental and basic identifiable changes in the conditions. Flexibility provides enough room for the manager to use his own discretion within the broad boundaries of the policy

3. It should be comprehensive in scope. It should be capable of being applied to different situations in a given area so that most cases can be handled at lower levels of the management, and only some exceptional cases, which are unique and are not covered by the policy are referred to the

higher management. For example, personnel policies should cover guidance for answering all questions that may arise in that area. These may be in reference to hiring, firing, promotions, transfers, training, remuneration, and so on.

4. A sound policy should be related to the objectives of the company and be in harmony with the economic, political, and social environment of the company. Policies are instruments for moving towards the objectives. Sound policies, understood by all, will leave little room for discontent and grievance, hence assisting in smooth operations necessary for achieving objectives. Additionally, if the law demands equal opportunities for all and society expects it, then the policy should be consistent with these requirements.

5. A sound policy should help coordinate multiple activities. Even though different work groups and divisions will have different functional policies, they must be bonded together with the common theme of the organizational goals. These sub-policies should not contradict each other.

6. A sound policy, not only prescribes general guidelines for conduct, but also establishes criteria for current and future action for a given set of circumstances and given decision variables, and methods and procedures for accomplishment.

7. It must be based on known principles, facts, and truth. For example, a policy, 'The customer is always right,' may be a good policy, but it is not based on truth. Similarly, a policy based on assumption that older people are less efficient, may not be based on facts and, hence, will not be a sound one.

8. A sound policy should establish the desired image of the company. Policies are useful indicators of the conduct and philosophy of the company and what the company stands for. These policies being formal statements can easily be communicated to the organizational members as well as the outside public.

While policies are pre-determined guideline that provides direction for decision-making purposes, procedures are the exact steps for an activity to be completed. Rules are specific and narrow guides to action. A rule needs to be followed strictly and is generally reinforced by penalties. All policies, procedures, rules and regulations, methods, and strategies are designed to implement and support the planning process so that the goals and objectives of the organization are achieved in an orderly way. Planning is a very important and critical ingredient of organizational operations and decision-making.

Process of Policy Formulation

Policy formulation is an important aspect of planning. The smooth working of an organization requires the formulation of policies.

1. Defining Policy Area:

The area for which a policy is to be framed should be defined. The objectives and needs of the organization should be kept in mind while specifying the policy area. While framing a marketing policy, the marketing expectations and thrust areas should be kept in mind. The scope of the policy will depend upon the area that it is supposed to cover. So the first thing in policy framing is to decide the area which it will cover.

2. Identifying Policy Alternatives:

The second step in policy formulation is the identification of policy alternatives. The alternatives should be decided based on an analysis of the external and internal environment. The internal environment will tell about the strengths and weaknesses of the organization while the external environment will reveal opportunities and levels of competition. Every alternative must ensure that the objective of the policy will be achieved.

3. Evaluating Alternatives:

All the alternatives are evolved in the light of organizational objectives. It should be analysed as to what contribution these alternatives will make in helping the organization for achieving its objectives. The factors like cost, benefits, and resource requirements of each alternative should be properly assessed. The effect of various alternatives on the environment of the organization should also be analyzed.

4. Selection of a Policy:

After proper evaluation, the most appropriate alternative is selected. The selection of a policy is a long-term commitment. In case the alternatives do not look satisfactory, then efforts should be made to develop other alternatives.

5. Trial Run of a Policy:

The policy should be implemented on a trial basis. It should be assessed if the policy is achieving the desired objectives. There may be suggestions during the test run, these should be used to modify the policy. Ultimately the policy should achieve the desired results otherwise a new policy alternative should be thought of.

6. Implementing Policy:

If the policy is finally alright it should be implemented. The policy should be explained to those who are to implement it. There should be a proper discussion about the implications and impact of various clauses or provisions of the policy. Proper communication of the purpose and objective of the policy will help it in its implementation.

Factors Influencing Policies

Policies are framed to help in smoothening the operations of a business. They are influenced both by internal and external factors.

1. Objectives and Strategies of the Organization:

All policies are framed to facilitate the achievement of objectives. The objectives and strategies fix the parameters within which the policies will operate. The policies should be consistent with the organizational goals and strategies.

2. Organisational Structure:

Organisational structure determines the levels of positions and fixes the authority and responsibility of employees. The implementation of policies will be influenced by the type of organisation structure. A policy will be consistent with the positions and authority roles in the organisation. Policy determination will certainly be influenced by organisational structures.

3. Available Resources:

The availability of resources such as human, financial, and physical facilities will influence the formulation of a policy. If a policy implementation requires more resources than are available in the organisation , then it will not be feasible. Rather the resources will fix the limits beyond which a policy cannot go.

4. Managerial Values:

Managers are the persons who are the prime movers of policies. The ethics and value systems of managers have a direct influence on the formation and implementation of policies. For example, if managers believe in honesty and truthfulness, then these things will be reflected in various policies framed by them.

5. Social Factors:

Several social factors also influence the policies of the organisation. If society wants only quality products, does not tolerate the exploitation of consumers, and gives importance to pollution control, all these factors will have to be taken into account while framing policies for the organisation.

6. Political Factors:

Political factors have a great influence on the policies of an organisation. The framework of business is determined by the party in power. The thinking of a political party will certainly be reflected in the industrial, fiscal, and monetary policies of the government. Every enterprise has to incorporate government policies into its policies. So political factors have a direct bearing on organisational policies.

Types of Policies

Every enterprise has several policies. Some of the types are discussed as follows:

1. Major Policies:

Major policies are those which give a unified direction to an enterprise and imply a commitment of resources. These policies give shape to an enterprise in the accomplishment of its purpose. They should also be supportive of the organisational objectives.

2. Supportive Policies:

Besides major policies, there is a need to have supportive policies also. Supportive policies are meant to help in the implementation of major policies. A concern may have the development of a new product as a major policy, the research to find out the unfulfilled needs of consumers may be a supportive policy.

3. Minor Policies:

The policies which do not influence the main objectives of the enterprise may be called minor policies. These policies may relate to some routine matters of less importance. A policy may be to hire casual workers in case of emergencies. A manager may allow workers to go on leave if the workload is less. The policies relating to such matters may be called minor policies. These policies do give directions but are not of much significance.

4. Composite Policies:

Some concerns have several policies or groups of policies. To increase sales, a concern may follow expansion, taking up of similar products, aggressive marketing, etc. To achieve one objective several policies may be used, these are composite policies.

STRATEGY V/S POLICIES

The strategy has often been used as a synonym for policy. However, both are different and should not be used interchangeably.

The policy is the guideline for decisions and actions on the part of subordinates. It is a general statement of understanding made for the achievement of objectives. Policies are statements or commonly accepted understandings of decision-making. They are thought-oriented. Power is delegated to the subordinates for the implementation of policies. In general terms, the policy is concerned with the course of action chosen for the fulfillment of the set objectives. It is an overall guide that governs and controls managerial actions.

Policies may be general or specific, organizational or functional, written or implied. They should be clear and consistent. Policies have to be integrated so that strategy is implemented successfully and effectively. For example, when the performance of two employees is similar, the promotion policy may require the promotion of the senior employee and hence he would be eligible for the promotion.

Strategies, on the other hand, are concerned with the direction in which human and physical resources are deployed and applied to maximize the chances of achieving organizational objectives in the face of environmental variables. Strategies are specific actions suggested to achieve the objectives. Strategies are action-oriented and everyone in the organization is empowered to implement them. Strategy cannot be delegated downward because it may require last-minute decisions.

Strategies and policies, both are the means to the end. In other words, both are directed toward meeting organizational objectives. Strategy is a rule for making decisions while the policy is a contingent decision.

DECISION MAKING

Decision-making is an integral part of modern management. Essentially, rational or sound decision-making is taken as the primary function of management. Decisions play important roles as they determine both organizational and managerial activities. A decision can be defined as a course of action purposely chosen from a set of alternatives to achieve organizational or managerial objectives or goals. The Decision-making process is a continuous and indispensable component of managing any organization or business activities. Decisions are made to sustain the activities of all business activities and organizational functioning. Decisions are made at every level of management to ensure organizational or business goals are achieved.

Definition of Decision Making

According to the Oxford Advanced Learner's Dictionary, the term decision making means - the process of deciding about something important, especially in a group of people or in an organization.

"Decision-making involves the selection of a course of action from among two or more possible alternatives to solve a given problem".

Decision-making process :

The decision-making process is a consultative affair done by a comity of professionals to drive the better functioning of any organization. Thereby, it is a continuous and dynamic activity that pervades all other activities of the organization. Since it is an ongoing activity, the decision-making process plays vital importance in the functioning of an organization. Since intellectual minds are involved in the process of decision-making, it requires solid scientific knowledge coupled with skills and experience in addition to mental maturity. Further, the decision-making process can be regarded as a check and balance system that keeps the organisation growing both in vertical and linear directions. It means that the decision-making process seeks a goal. The goals are pre-set business objectives, company missions, and its vision. To achieve these goals, the company may face a lot of obstacles in administrative, operational, marketing wings, and operational domains. Such problems are sorted out through a comprehensive decision-making process. No decision comes as end in itself, since it may evolve new problems to solve. When one problem is solved another arises and so on, such that the decision-making process, as said earlier, is continuous and dynamic.

A lot of time is consumed while decisions are taken. In a management setting, decisions cannot be taken abruptly. It should follow the steps such as

1. Defining the problem
2. Gathering information and collecting data
3. Developing and weighing the options
4. Choosing the best possible option
5. Plan and execute
6. Take follow-up action

Factors Affecting Decision-Making

Some of the factors and personal characteristics that have an impact on the decision maker are described below. Some factors are more important at higher levels of management and others are more important at lower levels.

Information inputs

It is very important to have adequate and accurate information about the situation for decision-making, otherwise, the quality of the decision will suffer. It must be recognized, however, that an individual has certain mental constraints which limit the amount of information that he can adequately handle. Less information is as dangerous as too much information. Some risk takers and highly authoritative individuals do make decisions on the basis of comparatively less information than more conservative decision makers.

Prejudice

Prejudice and bias is introduced in our decisions by our perceptual processes and may cause us to make ineffective decisions. First of all, perception is highly selective, which means that we only accept what we want to accept and hence our senses filter only such type of information. Secondly, perception is highly subjective, which means that information gets distorted in order to be consistent with our pre-established beliefs, attitudes, and values. For example, a preconceived idea that a given person or an organization is an honest or deceptive, a good or poor source of information, late or prompt on delivery, can have a considerable effect on the objective ability of the decision maker and the quality of the decision.

Cognitive constraints

The human brain, which is the source of all thinking, creativity and thus decisionmaking, is limited in capacity in a number of ways. For example, except in unique circumstances, our memory is short-term with the capacity of only a few ideas, words, and symbols. Secondly, we cannot perform more than a limited number of calculations in our heads which are not enough to compare all the possible alternatives in order to make an intelligent choice. Finally, psychologically, we are always uncomfortable with making decisions. We are never really sure if our choice of the alternative was correct and optimal until the impact of the implication of the decision has been felt. This makes us feel very insecure.

Attitudes about risk and uncertainty

These attitudes are developed in a person, partly due to certain personal characteristics and partly due to organizational characteristics. If the organizational policy is such that it penalizes losses more than it rewards gains, then the decision maker would tend to avoid such alternatives that have some chances of failure. Thus, a manager may avoid a potentially good opportunity if there is a slight chance of a loss. The personal characteristics of a decision maker regarding his attitude towards risk-taking affect the success of the decision. The risk-taking attitude is influenced by the following variables.

(i) Intelligence of the decision maker: Higher intelligence generally results in highly conservative attitudes and highly conservative decision-makers are low-risk takers. There are others who are more willing to take calculated risks if the potential rewards are large and there is some chance of success.

(ii) Expectations of the decision maker: People with high expectations are generally highly optimistic in nature and are willing to make decisions even with less information. The decision-makers with low expectations of success will require more and more information to decide upon a course of action.

(iii) Time constraints: As the complexity of the personal habits of the decision maker and the complexity of the decision variables increase, so does the time required to make a rational decision. Even though there are certain individuals who work best under time pressures and may outperform others under severe time constraints, most people, require time to gather all the available information for evaluation purposes. However, most people under time constraints rely on a 'heuristic approach', which relies on satisfactory decisions rather than optimal decisions, thus limiting the search for additional information, considering few alternatives and few characteristics of alternatives, and focusing on reasons to reject some alternatives. This approach may also be in use when the cost of gathering information and evaluating all such information is too high

CHAPTER IV

ORGANISING

The only way to excel is by knowing what role you play in a team operation and how one role relates to another. This applies to all fields, including business, government, cricket, and symphony orchestras. The administrative function of organising primarily consists of creating and maintaining these systems of responsibilities. Organizing involves coordinating and allocating a firm's resources to carry out its plans. It includes developing a structure for the people, positions, departments, and activities within the firm. Many people use the term "organisation" in a broad sense. Some argue that it includes all participant behaviour. Others would associate it with the entire web of social and cultural connections. Others refer to a company as an "organisation." Most managers, on the other hand, associate the term organisation with a formalised intentional structure of roles or positions.

The next phase is to coordinate the enterprise's activities to work on the plan and achieve the organisational objectives after the general and specific objectives have been established and achieved. The management must decide which tasks must be completed to achieve the goals, organise these tasks, and assign them to the departments. Organization entails assigning tasks to individuals whose efforts must be coordinated to realise predetermined goals and carry out predetermined tactics.

An organization is an entity such as a company or an association that consists of one or more people and has a specific purpose. The word is derived from the Greek word organ, meaning instrument or instrument, musical instrument and organ. An organization is a group of people who work together, like a neighborhood association, a charity, a union, or a corporation. Organization is also the act of forming or establishing something (like an organization).

An organization structure should be designed:

(a) to clarify who is to do what tasks and who is responsible for what results,

(b) to remove obstacles to performance caused by confusion and uncertainly of assignment, and

(c) to furnish decision-making and communication networks reflecting and supporting enterprise objectives.

DEFINITION

Organising can be defined as a process that initiates the implementation of plans by clarifying jobs, and working relationships and effectively deploying resources for the attainment of identified and desired results (goals).

According to Koontz and O'Donnell, "Organization involves the grouping of activities necessary to accomplish goals and plans, the assignment of these activities to appropriate departments and the provision of authority, delegation, and coordination."

Louis A. Allen defines organizing as "The process of identifying and grouping the work to be performed, defining and delegating responsibility and authority and establishing relationships to enable people to work most effectively together in accomplishing objectives".

"Organizing is determining what tasks are to be done, who is to do them, how the tasks are to be grouped, who reports to whom, and where decisions are to be made." – Stephen P. Robbins and Mary Coulter

<u>NATURE OR CHARACTERISTICS OF ORGANISING</u>

From the study of the various definitions given by different management experts, we get the following information about the characteristics or nature of the organisation

(1) Division of Work:

Division of work is the basis of an organization. In other words, there can be no organization without division of work. Under division of work, the entire work of business is divided into many departments. The work of every department is further sub-divided into sub-works. In this way, each individual has to do the saran work repeatedly which gradually makes that person an expert.

(2) Coordination:

Under organizing different persons are assigned different works but the aim of all these persons happens to be the same - the attainment of the objectives of the enterprise. The organization ensures that the work of all the persons depends on each other's work even though it happens to be different. The work of one person starts from where the work of another person ends. The non-completion of the work of one person affects the work of everybody. Therefore, everybody completes his work in time and does not hinder the work of others. It is thus, clear that it is like an organization to establish coordination among different works, departments, and posts in the enterprise.

(3)Plurality of Persons:

An organization is a group of many persons who assemble to fulfill a common purpose. A single individual cannot create an organization.

(4) Common Objectives:

There are various parts of an organization with different functions to perform but all move in the direction of achieving a general objective.

(5)Well-defined Authority and Responsibility:

Under organization, a chain is established between different posts right from the top to the bottom. It is specified as to what will be the authority and responsibility of every post. In other words, every individual working in the organization is given some authority for efficient work performance and it is also decided simultaneously as to what will be the responsibility of that individual in case of unsatisfactory work performance.

(6)Organization is a Structure of Relationship:

The relationship between persons working on different posts in the organization is decided. In other words, it is decided as to who will be the superior and who will be the subordinate. Leaving the top-level post and the lowest-level post everybody is somebody's superior and somebody's subordinate. The person working on the top level post has no superior and the person working on the lowest level post has no subordinate.

(7)Organization is a Machine of Management:

An organization is considered to be a machine of management because the efficiency of all the functions depends on an effective organization. In the absence of organization, no function can be performed in a planned manner. It is appropriate to call an organization a machine of management from another point of view. It is that machine in which no part can afford a tube ill-fitting or non-functional. In other words, if the division of work is not done properly or posts are not created correctly the whole system of management collapses.

(8)Organization is a Universal Process:

The organization is needed both in business and non-business organizations. Not only this, an organization will be needed where two or mom than two people work jointly. Therefore, the organization has the quality of universality.

(9)Organization is a Dynamic Process:

The organization is related to people and the knowledge and experience of the people change. The impact of this change affects the various functions of the organizations. Thus, the organization is not a process that can be decided for all times to come but it changes according to the needs. The example, in this case, can be the creation or abolition of a new post according to the need.

IMPORTANCE / ADVANTAGES OF ORGANIZING

The organization is an instrument that defines relations among different people which helps them to understand who happens to be their superior and who is their subordinate. This information helps in fixing responsibility and developing coordination. In such circumstances, the objectives of the organization can be easily achieved. That is why it is said that Organization is a mechanism of management. In addition to that, it helps in the other functions of management like planning, staffing, leading, controlling, etc. The importance of an organization or its merits becomes clear from the following facts,

(1) Increase In Managerial Efficiency:

A good and balanced organization helps the managers to increase their efficiency. Managers, through the medium of organization, make a proper distribution of the whole work among different people according to their ability.

(2) Proper Utilization of Resources:

Through the medium of organization optimum utilization of all the available human and material resources of an enterprise becomes possible. Work is allotted to every individual according to his ability and capacity and conditions and created to enable him to utilize his ability to the maximum extent. For example, if an employee possesses the knowledge of modem machinery but the modem machinery is not available in the organization, in that case, efforts are made to make available the modem machinery.

(3) Sound Communication Possible:

Communication is essential for making the right decision at the right time. However, the establishment of a good communication system is possible only through an organization. In an organization, the time of the communication is decided so that all the useful information reaches the officers concerned which in turn, helps the decision-making.

(4)Facilitates Coordination:

To attain successfully the objectives of the organization, coordination among various activities in the organization is essential. The organization is the only medium that makes coordination possible. Under organization, the division of work is made in such a manner as to make all the activities complementary to each other increasing their inter-dependence. Inter-dependence gives rise to the establishment of relations which, in turn, increases coordination.

(5)Increase in Specialization:

Under organization, the whole work is divided into different parts. Competent persons are appointed to handle all the sub-works and by taking a particular work repeatedly they become specialists. This enables them to have maximum work performance in the minimum time while the organization gets the benefit of specialization

(6)Helpful in Expansion:

A good organization helps the enterprise in facing competition. When an enterprise starts making available good-quality products at cheap rates, it increases the demand for its products. To meet the increasing demand for its products, an organization has to expand its business. On the other hand, a good organization has an element of flexibility that far from impeding the expansion work encourages it.

BASIS OF DEPARTMENTATION

There are six different bases of departmentation in an organization. The basis is:

1. Departmentation by Function
2. Departmentation by Products
3. Departmentation by Territory/Geographic Departmentation
4. Departmentation by Customers
5. Departmentation by Process
6. Combined Base.

1. Departmentation by Function:

Similar activities of a business are grouped into significant departments or divisions under an executive who reports to the chief executive. This departmentation is the most widely used basis for organising activities and is present in every organisation at some level

<u>Merits</u>

- It suits well small enterprises for creating major departments.
- It promotes specialization.

- It economizes operations and makes possible the adoption of logical and comprehensible structures.
- It facilitates interdepartmental coordination.
- It suits well those organisations which have a single product line.

<u>Demerits</u>

- It may lead to excessive centralization.
- The Decision-making process is delayed.
- Poor inter-departmental coordination.
- It is rather difficult to set up specific accountability and profit centers within functional departments so the performance is not accurately measured.
- It hinders human development in all

2. Departmentation by Product:

In a multiproduct organisation the departmentation by product most suits. Here the activities are grouped based on produce or product lines. All functions related to a particular product are bought together under the umbrella of the product manager.

<u>Merits</u>

- Each product division can be a viable profit center for accountability purposes. The performance of individual products can be easily accessed to distinguish between profitable and unprofitable products.
- Marketing strategy becomes more pragmatic.
- Top management is relieved of operating task responsibility and can concentrate on such centralized activities as finance, research, etc.
- It facilitates decentralization.
- Attention is given to product lines, which is good for further diversification and expansion.

<u>Demerits</u>

- It increases management costs. Service functions are duplicated both at the top and at the operating levels of management.
- The high cost of operation prevents the small & medium-sized concerns from adopting this basis of classification, particularly for creating major

units.

- There are problems at the top of coordination.

3. Departmentation by Territory:

It is suitable for organisations having a wide geographical market such as pharmaceuticals, banking, consumer goods, insurance, railways, etc. Here, the market is broken up into sales territories and a responsible executive is put in charge of each territory. The territory may be known as a district, division, or region.

<u>Merits</u>

- It helps in achieving the benefits of local operations such as a local supply of materials & labour, local markets, etc.
- Full attention can be paid to local customer groups.
- A regional division achieves better coordination and supervision of activities in a particular area.
- It helps in reducing transportation and distribution costs.
- It facilitates the expansion of business to different regions.
- It provides an opportunity for a regional manager to gain broad experience as he looks after the complete operation in a particular territory

<u>Demerits</u>

- It creates the problem of communication and coordination between various regional offices.
- It may be uneconomical due to costly duplication of personnel & physical facilities.
- It may be difficult to provide efficient centralized services to various departments located in different areas.
- The problem of top management control becomes difficult.

4. Departmentation by Customers:

This type of classification is adopted by enterprises offering specialized services. To give attention to heterogeneous groups of buyers in the market, marketing activities are often split into various several parts. Such groups are suitable for organisations serving several segments like a pharmaceutical company supplying to institutional buyers such as hospitals and government and non-institutional buyers such as wholesalers and retail chemists.

Merits

- The main advantage of following this type of departmentation is that particular needs of the particular- customers can be solved.
- Benefits of specialization can be obtained.

Demerits

- There may be duplication and underutilization of facilities and resources.
- It may be difficult to maintain coordination among the different customer departments.

Thus, customer departmentation is useful for those enterprises which have to cater to the special and varied needs of different classes of customers.

5. Departmentation by Process:

The production function may be further subdivided based on the process of production when the production process has distinct activity groups, they are taken as the basis of departmentation. Process departmentation is suitable when the machines or equipment used are costly and required special skills for operating. It is useful for organisations that are engaged in the manufacture of products that involves several processes.

Merits

- It provides economy of operation
- The benefits of specialization are available.
- Efficient maintenance of equipment is possible.
- It simplifies supervision and plant layout.

Demerits

- There may be difficulties in coordinating the activities of different departments
- Due to specialized activity, employee mobility is reduced.

- Extreme specialization may reduce the flexibility of operations.

This type of departmentation may not provide an opportunity for the all-around development of managerial talent.

6. Departmentation-combined base:

Combined base departmentation is also called composite departmentation or mixed departmentation. This type of departmentation provides the benefits of both functional and product structures. But the conflicts between different departments and divisions may increase. It becomes necessary to differentiate clearly between the line authority and functional authority of managers.

SPAN OF MANAGEMENT

The span of control is also known as the span of management or the span of supervisor and span of authority. A manager cannot supervise the activities of an unlimited number of people. It is an important principle that states that there should be a manageable number of subordinates under one superior. The span of control refers to the number of subordinates a manager can supervise effectively. The Span of Management refers to the number of subordinates who can be managed efficiently by a superior. Simply, the manager has a group of subordinates who report to him directly is called the span of management.

Factors determining Span of Management

The span of management can be determined based on several relationships that a manager can manage. These are:

i. Capacity of Superior

The capacity of a manager to manage, i.e., planning and decision-making, leading and motivating, communicating, controlling, etc., affects the span of management. A manager with more managerial capacity can manage more subordinates in a given situation. In the same way, a manager's attitudes and personality aspects do affect the span of management.

ii. Capacity of Subordinates

Efficient and trained subordinates discharge their functions efficiently without much help from their superiors. They only need broad guidelines. In such a case, the span may be larger because a superior will be required to devote less time to managing them. This means a superior can manage a large number of subordinates as he will be required just to give the broad guidelines and devote less time to each.

iii. Degree of Centralisation

The degree of centralisation (or decentralisation) affects the degree of the superior's involvement in decision-making. The rule is:- The higher the degree of decentralisation, the higher the span of management, and vice versa. In a centralised working pattern, a superior is required to spare more time and energy as subordinates require frequent and considerable consultation, clarification, instruction, etc., and the span of management contracts.

iv. Degree in Planning

A superior's workload is significantly reduced when subordinates carry out precisely prepared (or well-planned) activities. Well-planned activities increase the range of control in comparison to unplanned actions. When everything is specified explicitly, subordinates can complete their tasks without the direct supervision of their superiors.

v. Communication Techniques

As against face-to-face personal communication, the use of staff assistance with electronic media (like phone, fax, e-mail, intercom, and so forth) can expand the span of control. Personal communication requires a superior to spare more time and it decreases the span of control.

vi. Staff Assistance

The use of staff assistance in reducing the workload of managers enables them to manage more number of subordinates. Many of the managerial functions can be discharged by these staff personnel on behalf of the managers. They can collect information, process communications, and issue orders and instruction on behalf of their superiors. This process saves time for managers and the degree of span can be increased.

vii. Supervision from Others

The classical approach to the span of management, i.e., each person should have a single supervisor is changing these days. Now the subordinates are being supervised by other managers in the organization such as staff personnel. This has helped the manager to have a large number of subordinates under him.

Types of Organization

There are two broad categories of organisation, which are:

1. Formal Organisation

2. Informal Organisation

Formal Organisation: Formal organisation is that type of organisation structure where the authority and responsibility are clearly defined. The organisation structure has a defined delegation of authority and roles and responsibilities for the members.

The formal organisation has predefined policies, rules, schedules, procedures, and programs. The decision-making activity in a formal organisation is mostly based on predefined policies.

A formal organisation structure is created by the management with the objective of attaining the organisational goals.

There are several types of formal organisation based on their structure, which are discussed as follows:

1. Line Structure Organization: – Line structure organization is the simplest and oldest form of organization structure. It is called a scalar type of military or divisional organization. Under this system, authority flows directly and vertically downward from the top of the managerial hierarchy to different levels of managers and subordinates, and down to the operative level of workers. It is also known as the chain of command or scalar principle.

2. Line and Staff Organization: – Line and staff organization, in management, approach authorities (For example: – managers) to establish goals and instructions that are then met by employees and other workers. A line and staff organizational structure attempt to present a large and complex enterprise in a more flexible way without sacrificing managerial authority. Staff groups support those who are engaged in the central productive activity of the enterprise. They back up their work. Staff groups help the organisation in analysing, researching, counselling, monitoring, and evaluating activities.

3. Functional Structure Organization: – Functional Structure Organization is one of the most common structures of organization. They are grouped based on their specific skills and knowledge. Under this structure, the employees are divided into groups by the organization according to a particular group of tasks. Where functional structures operate well in stable environments, where business strategies have little inclination for change or mobility, the level of bureaucracy makes it difficult for organizations to react quickly to market changes.

4. Matrix Structure Organization: – A matrix organizational structure is a structure of organization in which some individuals report to more than one supervisor or leader, which is described as a solid line or dotted line reporting. More broadly, it can also describe the management of cross-functional, cross-business groups and other work models that do not maintain rigid business units or silos grouped by function and geography. For example, an employee may have a primary manager they report to as well as one or more project managers they work under.

<u>5. Project Structure Organization</u>: – A project structure organizational structure is used to determine the hierarchy and authority of people involved in a specific project. This organizational structure is temporarily created for specific projects for a particular period, for the project to achieve the goal of developing a new product, specialize in various functional departments such as production, engineering, quality control, marketing research, etc. and will be ready to work together. These specialists return to their duties as soon as the project is completed.

In fact, the project organization is established with the aim of overcoming the major weakness of functional organization, such as the absence of unity of command, delay in decision making, and lack of coordination.

Informal Organisation: Informal organisations are those types of organisations that do not have a defined hierarchy of authority and responsibility. In such organisations, the relationship between employees is formed based on common interests, preferences, and prejudices.

CHAPTER V

DIRECTING & CONTROLLING

Directing is the heart of management functions. It is the process of integrating the people within the organisation so as to obtain their willing co-operation towards meeting the pre-determined goals. Direction is an aspect of management that deals directly with influencing, guiding, supervising, and motivating staff for the achievement of organizational goals. All other functions of management such as planning, organizing, and staffing have no importance without directing. Leadership, motivation, supervision, and communication are various aspects of directing.

The process or technique of instructing, guiding, inspiring, counselling, supervising, and leading people to achieve organisational goals is referred to as direction. It is a continuous managerial process that occurs throughout the organization's existence.

According to Theo Haimann," Directing consists of the process and techniques utilized in issuing instructions and making certain that operations are carried on as originally planned."

Principles of Direction:

The following are the basic principles of directing:

1. Integration of individual and organizational goals: This implies that the individua ls contribute to the organizational goals to their maximum capabilities and at the same time satisfy their personal needs.

2. Participative decision making: Effective direction can be achieved by involving individuals and groups in decision making process.

3. Delegation of Authority: The subordinates should be delegated with adequate authority in order to facilitate decision making.

4. Effective communication: The managers should ensure free flow of communication at all levels of organizational hierarchy.

5. Right type of leadership: The management should develop leadership quality among the employees.

6. Unity of Command: This principle states that the subordinates should get directives from one superior only and should be accountable to one superior only.

7. Appropriateness of direction techniques: The direction techniques selected should be according to the situation.

8. Follow up: The management should see that whether the direction issued by them is carried out or not. In simple words, the direction can be described as providing guidance to workers for doing work.

Techniques of Direction

There are mainly three techniques are used for direction:

1. Consultative direction: Under this method, the supervisor has a consultation with his subordinates before issuing a direction. The consultation is made to find out the feasibility, enforceability, and nature of the problem.

2. Free rein direction: Under these techniques, the subordinate is encouraged to solve the problem independently. The subordinate should take initiative to solve the problem.

3. Autocratic direction: It is opposite to free rein direction. The supervisor commands his subordinates and has close supervision over them.

MOTIVATION

Motivation is the process of channelling a person's inner drives so that he wants to accomplish the goals of the organization. Motivation concerns itself with the will to work. It seeks to know the incentives for the work and tries to find out the ways and means whereby their realization can be helped and encouraged. Motivation is a Latin word which means 'to move'. Human motives are internalized goals within individuals. Motivation may be defined as those forces that cause people to behave in certain ways.

According to Louis Allen, "motivation is the work of a manager performs to inspire, encourage and impel people to take required action" In the words of William G Scott, "motivation means a process of stimulating people to action to accomplish desired goals" Thus motivation is a process by which a need or desire is aroused and a psychological force within our mind sets us in motion to fulfill our needs and desires. An unsatisfied need becomes the motive for a person to spend his energy in order to achieve a goal.

Characteristics of Motivation

The following are the important characteristics and nature of motivation

1. Motivation is an internal feeling – Motivation is a psychological phenomenon which is a force within an individual that drives him to behave in a certain way.

2. Motivation produces goal-directed behaviour – An individual's behaviour is directed towards a goal.

3. Motivation is related to needs – Needs are deficiencies that are created whenever there is a physiological or psychological imbalance.

4. Motivation can be positive or negative – Positive or incentive motivation is generally based on rewards. Negative or fear motivation is based on force and fear.

5. Motivation is a continuous process – Satisfaction of human needs is a never-ending process. It is a continuous process. So motivation is also a continuous process.

6. Motivation is dynamic – The needs of a person today may be different from the needs of tomorrow. So motivation is highly dynamic.

Importance and benefits of Motivation

Motivation is an effective device in the hands of a manager for inspiring the workforce and creating confidence in it. By motivating the workforce, management can achieve the organizational goals. The various benefits of motivation are

1. A manager directs or guides the workers' actions in the desired direction for accomplishing the goals of the organization by motivating the workers.

2. Workers will try to be efficient as possible by improving upon their skills and knowledge so that they are able to contribute to the progress of the organization.

3. Ability to work and willingness to work are necessary for performing any task. These two things can be created only by motivation.

4. Motivation contributes to good industrial relations in the organization.

5. Motivation is the best remedy for resistance to changes. If the workers of an organization are motivated, they will accept any change whole-heartily for the organizational benefits.

6. Motivation facilitates the maximum utilization of all the factors of production and thereby contributes to higher production.

7. Motivation promotes a sense of belonging among the workers.

8. Motivation leads to lower turnover and absenteeism because a satisfied employee will not leave the organization.

LEADERSHIP

A leader is someone who has the capacity to create a compelling vision that takes people to a new place, and to translate that vision into action. Leaders draw other people to them by enrolling them in their vision. What a leader does is inspire people and empower them. Thus a leader is a person who has a vision, a drive and a commitment to achieve that vision, and the skills to make it happen.

Leadership is an activity on the part of the managers to get something done by others, willingly and not by compulsion. Leadership is a process of influence on a group. It is the ability of a manager to induce subordinates to work with confidence.

In the words of Koontz and O' Donnel, "leadership is the ability of a manager to induce subordinates to work with confidence and zeal."

According to Chester I Bernard, "leadership refers to the quality of the behaviour of individuals whereby they guide people on their activities in organized efforts"

Thus leadership is a psychological process of influencing followers and providing guidance, directing, and leading the people in an organization towards the attainment of the objectives of the enterprise.

Nature or Characteristics of Leadership

1. A leader should have followers

2. Leadership is basically a personal quality

3. Leadership involves a community of interest between the leader and his followers

4. Leadership is a process of influence

5. leadership is the function of stimulation

6. A leader ensures absolute justice

7. Leadership is a continuous, dynamic, and ever-evolving process.

Leadership Styles

The term leadership style can be defined as a leader's behaviour towards group members. It refers to the pattern of behaviour which a leader adopts in influencing the behaviour of his subordinates in the organizational context. Different leadership styles can be categorized as follows.

1. Autocratic Leadership: Autocratic leadership is also known as an authoritarian, directive, leader-centered or monothetic style. Under this style, the leader concentrates all authority on himself, instructs a subordinate as to what to do, how to do it, when to do it, etc. He also

exercises close supervision and control over his subordinates. There are three categories of autocratic leaders

a. Strict Autocrat – A strict autocrat relies on negative influence and gives orders which the subordinates must accept. He may also use his powers to disperse rewards to his group.

b. Benevolent Autocrat – The benevolent is effected in getting high productivity in many situations and he can develop effective human relationship. His motivational style is usually positive.

c. Manipulative Autocrat – A manipulative autocrat leader is one who makes the subordinates feel that they are participating in decision making process even though he has already taken the decisions.

2. Participative Leadership: This style is also called a democratic, consultative, group-centered, or ideographic style. A participative leader is one who consults and invites his subordinates to participate in the decision-making process. Under this style, subordinates are freely allowed to communicate with the leader and also with their fellow subordinates and take their own initiative.

3. Laissez Faire or Free-rein Leadership: Under this style of leadership, the leader largely depends upon the group and its members to establish their own goals and make their own decisions. The leader is passive and assumes the role of just another member of the group. Only very little control is exercised over group members. This style is also known permissive style of leadership. This style is suitable for certain situations where the manager can leave a choice to his groups.

Qualities of a successful leader

The following are the major innate qualities in a successful leader.

- Physical appearance- A leader must have a pleasing appearance. Physique and health are very important for a good leader.
- Vision and foresight- A leader cannot maintain influence unless he exhibits that he is forward-looking. He has to visualize situations and thereby has to frame logical programs.
- Intelligence- A leader should be intelligent enough to examine problems and difficult situations. He should be analytical weighs the pros and cons and then summarizes the situation. Therefore, a positive bent of mind and mature outlook is very important.
- Communicative skills- A leader must be able to communicate the policies and procedures clearly, precisely, and effectively. This can be

helpful in persuasion and stimulation.

- Objective- A leader has to be having a fair outlook that is free from bias and which does not reflects his willingness towards a particular individual. He should develop his own opinion and should base his judgment on facts and logic.

- Knowledge of work- A leader should very precisely know the nature of the work of his subordinates because it is then he can win the trust and confidence of his subordinates.

- Sense of responsibility- Responsibility and accountability towards an individual's work are very important to bring a sense of influence. A leader must have a sense of responsibility toward organizational goals because only then he can get maximum capabilities exploited in a real sense. For this, he has to motivate himself and arouse an urge to give the best of his abilities. Only then he can motivate the subordinates to be the best.

- Self-confidence and willpower- Confidence in himself is important to earn the confidence of the subordinates. He should be trustworthy and should handle the situations with full willpower.

- Humanist-This trait to be present in a leader is essential because he deals with human beings and is in personal contact with them. He has to handle the personal problems of his subordinates with great care and attention. Therefore, treating human beings on humanitarian grounds is essential for building a congenial environment.

- Empathy- It is an old adage "Stepping into the shoes of others". This is very important because fair judgment and objectivity come only then. A leader should understand the problems and complaints of employees and should also have a complete view of the needs and aspirations of the employees. This helps in improving human relations and personal contact with the employees

COMMUNICATION

Communication is a process in which Information, Ideas, Thoughts, and Feelings are exchanged between two or more people. It is a process of sending and receiving information between two or more people. The person who is sending a message is referred to as the sender, while a person who is receiving information is known as a receiver.

Types of Communication

People communicate with each other in different ways that depend on the message. There are two types of communication are:

1. Verbal Communication

2. Non-Verbal Communication

Verbal Communication

Verbal communication refers to that communication in which a message is transmitted verbally. It can be done by words of mouth and a piece of writing. When we talk to others, we assume that others understand what we are saying because we know what we are saying. But this is not the case. Usually, people bring their own attitudes, perception, emotions, and thoughts about the topic and hence creating a barrier to delivering the right meaning.

It can be divided into two forms: Oral Communication, Written Communication

Oral Communication -Oral Communication is that communication which formed orally like spoken words. It includes face-to-face conversation, speech, telephonic conversation, videos, radio, and television. It can be influenced by pitch, volume, speed, and clarity of speaking.

Written Communication -Written communication has great significance in today's business world. It is an innovative activity of the mind. Effective written communication is essential for preparing worthy promotional materials for business development. The speech came before writing. But writing is more unique and formal than speech. Effective writing involves careful choice of words, their organization in the correct order in sentence formation as well as the cohesive composition of sentences. Also, writing is more valid and reliable than speech.

Nonverbal Communication

Nonverbal communication is the sending or receiving of wordless messages. We can say that communication other than oral and written, such as gesture, body language, posture, tone of voice, or facial expressions, is called nonverbal communication. Nonverbal communication is all about the body language of the speaker. Nonverbal communication helps the receiver in interpreting the message received. Often, nonverbal signals reflect the situation more accurately than verbal messages. Sometimes nonverbal response contradicts verbal communication and hence affects the effectiveness of the message.It involves appearance, body language, and Sound.

There are two types of communication are:

1. Formal Communication

2. Informal Communication

<u>Formal Communication</u>: In formal communication, certain rules, conventions, and principles are followed while communicating the message. Formal communication occurs in a formal and official style. Usually, professional settings, corporate meetings, and conferences undergo in formal pattern. In formal communication, the use of slang and foul language is avoided and correct pronunciation is required. Authority lines are needed to be followed in formal communication.

<u>Informal Communication</u>: Informal communication is done using channels that are in contrast with formal communication channels. It's just casual talk. It is established for societal affiliations of members in an organization and face-to-face discussions. It happens among friends and family. In informal communication use of slang words, and foul language is not restricted. Usually, Informal communication is done orally and using gestures. Informal communication, Unlike formal communication, doesn't follow authority lines. In an organization, it helps in finding out staff grievances as people express more when talking informally. Informal communication helps in building relationships. An informal channel of communication is also known as Grape wine.

Downward communication

Communication that flows from the superior to subordinates is referred as downward communication. It is needed,

- To get things done
- To prepare for changes
- To discourage misinformation and suspicion
- To let the people feel the price of being relatively well informed.

Upward communication

It flows from a subordinate position to a superior position. That is, the subordinate work performance report, their opinions, ideas and suggestions, complaints and grievances of subordinates, etc

PROCESS OF COMMUNICATION

Communication is a process of exchanging verbal and non-verbal messages. It is a continuous process. communication is a two-way process and is incomplete without feedback from the recipient to the sender on how well the message is understood by him.

1. Sender / Encoder – Sender / Encoder is a person who sends the message. A sender makes use of symbols (words or graphic or visual aids) to convey the message and produce the required response. For instance – a training manager conducting training for a new batch of employees. A sender may be an individual or a group or an organization. The views, background, approach, skills, competencies, and knowledge of the sender have a great impact on the message.

2. Message –A message is a key idea that the sender wants to communicate. It is a sign that elicits the response of the recipient. The communication process begins with deciding about the message to be conveyed. It must be ensured that the main objective of the message is clear.

3. Medium – Medium is a means used to exchange/transmit the message. The choice of an appropriate medium of communication is essential for making the message effective and correctly interpreted by the recipient. This choice of communication medium varies depending upon the features of communication. For instance – A written medium is chosen when a message has to be conveyed to a small group of people, while an oral medium is chosen when spontaneous feedback is required from the recipient as misunderstandings are cleared then and there.

4. Recipient / Decoder – A recipient / Decoder is a person for whom the message is intended/aimed/targeted. The degree to which the decoder understands the message is dependent upon various factors such as the knowledge of the recipient, their responsiveness to the message, and the reliance of the encoder on the decoder.

5. Feedback – Feedback is the main component of the communication process as it permits the sender to analyze the efficacy of the message. It helps the sender in confirming the correct interpretation of the message by the decoder. Feedback may be verbal (through words) or nonverbal (in form of smiles, sighs, etc.). It may take written form also in form of memos, reports, etc.

Barriers to Effective Communication

1. Physical Barriers: this has to do with poor or outdated equipment used during communications, background noise, poor lighting, and temperatures that are too hot or too cold.

2. Attitudes: emotions like anger or sadness can taint objectivity. Also being extremely nervous, having a personal agenda, or "needing to be right no matter what" can make communications less than effective. This is also

known as "Emotional Noise".

3. Language: this can seem like an easy one, but even people speaking the same language can have difficulty understanding each other if they are from different generations or from different regions of the same country. Slang, professional jargon, and regional colloquialisms can even hurt communicators with the best intentions.

4. Physiological Barriers: ill health, poor eyesight or hearing difficulties, pain.

5. Problems with Structure Design: companies or institutions can have organizational structures that are not clear, which can make communications difficult. Also to blame for faulty communications are bad information systems, and lack of supervision or training of the people involved.

6. Cultural Noise: people sometimes make stereotypical assumptions about others based on their cultural background.

7. Lack of Common Experience: it's a great idea to use examples or stories to explain a point that is being discussed. However, if the speaker and the audience cannot relate to these examples because they do not have the same knowledge or have not shared the same experiences then this tool will be ineffective.

8. Ambiguity and Abstractions Overuse: leaving things half-said, using too many generalizations, proverbs or sayings, can all lead to communications that are not clear and that can lend themselves to misinterpretations.

9. Information Overload: it takes time to process a lot of information and too many details can overwhelm and distract the audience from the important topics. Keep it Simple, Sweetie.

10. Assumptions and Jumping to Conclusions: This can make someone reach a decision about something before listening to all the facts.

11. Psychological barriers can be described as the cause of distorted communication because of human psychology problems. Psychological barriers may be ; Attitude and opinions, Emotions, Filtering and distortion of the message, Status difference, In attention, Closed mind, Fields of experience.

CO-ORDINATION

It is a process of integrating the interdepartmental activities as unified action towards the fulfilment of the predetermined common goals of the organization.

According to Henry Fayol, " To co-ordinate is to harmonize all the activities of concern so as to facilitate its working and its success. In a well co-ordinated enterprise, each department or division, works in harmony with other and is fully informed of its role in the organization. The working schedule of various departments is constantly turned to circumstances."

Features

1. It is not a separate function of management.

2. It is necessary for all levels of management.

3. It is a continuous and dynamic process.

4. Group efforts are more relevant than individual efforts.

5. Unity of action is the heart of co-ordination.

6. It is a system concept.

Types of Co-ordination

The following are the important types of co-ordination.

1. Vertical co-ordination: - It refers to co-ordination between the activities of a manager and his subordinates

2. Horizontal co-ordination:- It refers to co-ordination among peers – ie employees working at the same levels in organizational hierarchy and among various departments.

3. Diagonal co-ordination: It is co-ordination among the users and between users and service personnel, which is achieved through understanding, negotiation and voluntary effort.

Principles of Co-ordination:

In order to ensure effective co-ordination, the co-ordination should be based on certain principles:

1. Personal contact: Effective co-ordination can be achieved through personal contact. Personal contact avoids controversy and misunderstanding.

2. Reciprocal relationship: This principle says that all factors in a situation are reciprocally related. Each factor influences another factor.

3. Dynamism: Co-ordination is modified according to the external and internal actions and decisions ie co-ordination should be a dynamic one.

4. Continuity: It says that co-ordination is a continuous process.

5. Self co-ordination: According to this principle, the function of one department affects other departments and in turn, is affected by the

function of other departments.

6. Clear-cut objectives: As per this principle, the department heads should know clearly the objectives of the organization.

7. Effective communication: Effective communication is very necessary for the proper co- ordination.

8. Early stage of starting: The co-ordination should be started even from the planning function of management.

TECHNIQUES OF EFFECTIVE COORDINATION IN ORGANIZATION

Some of the techniques that are used to achieve effective coordination are given below:

1. Direct Contact: One of the most effective means of achieving coordination is direct contact. Written communication, modern electronic, mechanical devices, etc., can also be used.

2. Group Meetings: Group meetings are said to be an effective means of achieving coordination. At the time of meeting, superior comes into personal contact with those connected with the actual problems. Such meetings encourage the people to integrate their efforts. Coordination can be achieved through regular meetings of superiors and subordinates.

3. Organizational Structure: Coordination can be achieved only when the authority and responsibility of each and every person are clearly defined. In other words, the organizational structure should be designed properly so as to permit coordination among various activities along the line itself.

4. Effective Communication: In achieving coordination, effective communication plays a vital role. Communication greatly helps in coordination. The purpose of communication is to promote deep understanding among members by bringing and maintaining coordination in order to achieve the ultimate goals.

5. Committees: In order to coordinate the various activities, various types of committees may be appointed. Committees provide the means for synchronizing various efforts. Committees develop better understanding and morale among the members. They are greatly advisory in nature and make use of the best efforts of the members.

6. Staff Meetings: Staff meetings at regular intervals help in achieving effective coordination because such meetings provides opportunities for frank discussions and better exchange of ideas of people from different sections. This infuse a feeling of unity among the members which makes them to jointly work for the organization.

7. Effective Leadership: Leader inculcates a feeling of collectivism in the employees and forces them to work as a team. Individuals within the group may possess varied interests and multiple goals. Leader reconciles these conflicting goals and restores equilibrium. A good leader can achieve coordination at all stages. Hence, effective leadership is essential for achieving coordination.

8. Informal Coordination: Many organizations adopt informal means of coordination through processes of social, unofficial interactions, relationship and mutual adjustments. They are very often more effective than formal means.

CONTROLLING

The Control function is closely related to all other functions of management. Management control is the process of ensuring that the actual plan implementation matches with the original plan. It is an ongoing and dynamic function and linked with other functions of the management in a circular relationship. Definition According to KoontsO'Donnel, "Controlling is the measurement of accomplishment against the standards and the correction of deviation to assure attainment of objectives according to plan."

Steps in Control Process

The control process involves four basic steps as mentioned below:-

1. Establishing standards:- Standard represents criteria of performance. This implies the statement of goals and objectives envisaged under the planning process are stated in clear and measurable terms along with specific milestones. The standard should have some characteristics to produce effective performance.

2. Measurement of performance against standards: The measurement of performance is an ongoing process. Several techniques are used by the management to measure performance.

3. Comparing the actual performances with standards: The measured results are compared with the project and standards. In case the performance meets the standards, then it would mean that the performance or activity is progressing in the desired direction.

4. Taking corrective action: In the situations when performance does not confirm the specified criteria of the standards, then it is necessary to take corrective measures to deal with the observed deviations in the

performance.

CONTROL TECHNIQUES

- **Financial controls** : Financial audits, or formal investigations, are regularly conducted to ensure that financial management practices follow generally accepted procedures, policies, laws, and ethical guidelines. Audits may be conducted internally or externally.
- **Budget controls** : A budget depicts how much an organization expects to spend (expenses) and earn (revenues) over a time period. Amounts are categorized according to the type of business activity or account, such as telephone costs or sales of catalogs. Budgets not only help managers plan their finances but also help them keep track of their overall spending.Some budget development methods are as follows:

1. Top-down budgeting: Managers prepare the budget and send it to subordinates.
2. Bottom-up budgeting: Figures come from the lower levels and are adjusted and coordinated as they move up the hierarchy.
3. Zero-based budgeting: Managers develop each new budget by justifying the projected allocation against its contribution to departmental or organizational goals.
4. Flexible budgeting: Any budget exercise can incorporate flexible budgets, which set "meet or beat" standards that can be compared to expenditures.

- **Break Even Analysis:** Break Even Analysis or Break Even Point is the point of no profit, no loss. It means that any sale below this point will cause losses and any sale above this point will earn profits. The Break-even analysis acts as a control device. It helps to find out the company's performance. So the company can take collective action to improve its performance in the future. Break-even analysis is a simple control tool.
- **PERT and CPM Techniques**: Programme Evaluation and Review Technique (PERT) and Critical Path Method (CPM) techniques were developed in USA in the late 50's. Any programme consists of various activities and sub-activities. Successful completion of any activity depends upon doing the work in a given sequence and in a given time. CPM / PERT can be used to minimise the total time or the total cost required to perform the total operations. Importance is given to

identifying the critical activities. Critical activities are those which have to be completed on time otherwise the full project will be delayed. So, in these techniques, the job is divided into various activities / sub-activities. From these activities, the critical activities are identified. More importance is given to the completion of these critical activities. So, by controlling the time of the critical activities, the total time and cost of the job are minimised.

- **Management Audit**: Management Audit is an evaluation of the management as a whole. It critically examines the full management process, i.e. planning, organising, directing, and controlling. It finds out the efficiency of the management. To check the efficiency of the management, the company's plans, objectives, policies, procedures, personnel relations and systems of control are examined very carefully. Management auditing is conducted by a team of experts. They collect data from past records, members of management, clients and employees. The data is analysed and conclusions are drawn about managerial performance and efficiency.

- **Management Information System (MIS)**: In order to control the organisation properly the management needs accurate information. They need information about the internal working of the organisation and also about the external environment. Information is collected continuously to identify problems and find out solutions. MIS collects data, processes it and provides it to the managers. MIS may be manual or computerised. With MIS, managers can delegate authority to subordinates without losing control.

- **Computers and information controls** :Almost all organizations have confidential and sensitive information that they don't want to become general knowledge. Controlling access to computer databases is the key to this area. Increasingly, computers are being used to collect and store information for control purposes. Many organizations privately monitor each employee's computer usage to measure employee performance, among other things. Some people question the appropriateness of computer monitoring. Managers must carefully weigh the benefits against the costs—both human and financial—before investing in and implementing computerized control techniques.

- **Return on Investment (ROI)**: Investment consists of fixed assets and working capital used in business. Profit on the investment is a reward for risk taking. If the ROI is high then the financial performance of a business is good and vice-versa. ROI is a tool to improve financial performance. It helps the business to compare its present performance with that of previous years' performance. It helps to conduct inter-firm comparisons. It also shows the areas where corrective actions are needed.

CHAPTER VI

STAFFING

The human resource is one of the greatest for every organization because in any organization all other resources like- money, material, machine, etc. can be utilized effectively and efficiently through the positive efforts of human resources.

Therefore, it is very important that each and every person should get the right position in the organization so as to get the right job, according to their ability, talent, aptitude, and specializations so that it will help the organization to achieve the pre-set goals in the proper way by the 100% contribution of manpower.

Staffing is the process of recruiting employees who are eligible for certain positions in a company. Staffing means the process of filling and keeping various roles in an organisation filled. In management, it means the process of recruiting the right person at the right place to increase the efficiency of the organisation. An enterprise with an efficient workforce cannot function properly, so staffing helps an enterprise to acquire a workforce.

Steps involved in the staffing process

1. Manpower Planning: Manpower planning can be regarded as the quantitative and qualitative measurement of labour force required in an enterprise. Therefore, in an overall sense, the planning process involves the synergy in creating and evaluating the manpower inventory and as well as in developing the required talents among the employees selected for promotion advancement

2. Recruitment: Recruitment is a process of searching for prospective employees and stimulating them to apply for jobs in the organization. It stands for finding the source from which potential employees will be selected.

3. Selection: Selection is a process of eliminating those who appear unpromising. The purpose of this selection process is to determine whether a candidate is suitable for employment in the organization or not. Therefore, the main aim of the process of selection is to select the right candidates to fill various positions in the organization. A well-planned selection procedure is of utmost importance.

4. Placement: Placement means putting the person on the job for which he is selected. It includes introducing the employee to his job.

5. Training: After the selection of an employee, the important part of the program is to provide training to the new employee. With the various technological changes, the need for training employees is being increased to keep the employees in touch with the various new developments.

6. Development: A sound staffing policy provides for the introduction of a system of planned promotion in every organization. If employees are not at all have suitable opportunities for their development and promotion, they get frustrated which affects their work.

7. Promotion: The process of promotion implies the up-gradation of an employee to a higher post involving increasing rank, prestige and responsibilities. Generally, the promotion is linked to an increment in wages and incentives, but it is not essential that it always relates to that part of an organization.

8. Transfer: Transfer means the movement of an employee from one job to another without increment in pay, status, or responsibilities. Therefore, this process of staffing needs to be evaluated on a timely basis.

9. Appraisal: Appraisal of employees as to how efficiently the subordinate is performing a job and also to know his aptitudes and other qualities necessary for performing the job assigned to him

10. Determination of Remuneration: This is the last process which is very crucial as it involves determining remuneration which is one of the most difficult functions of the personnel department because there are no definite or exact means to determine correct wages

Benefits of Staffing Process

1. The staffing process helps in getting the right people for the right job at right time. The function of staffing helps the management to decide the number of employees needed for the organization and with what qualifications and experience.

2. The staffing process helps to improve organizational productivity. Therefore, through proper selection of employees in the organization, it can increase the quality of the employees, and through proper training, the performance level of the employees can also be improved.

3. It helps in providing job satisfaction to the employees and thus keeps their morale high. With proper training and development programs, the employees get motivation and their efficiency improves and they feel

assured of their career advancements.

4. It maintains harmony in the organization. Therefore with an overall performance of proper staffing in an organization, the individuals are not only recruited and selected but as a result, their performance is regularly appraised and promotions made on merit which fosters harmony and peace in the organization for the accomplishment of overall objectives of an organization.

Human Resource Management

Human resource is a very broad term with which an organisation or other human system describes the combination of traditionally administrative personnel functions with the acquisition and application of skills, knowledge, and experience, employee relations, and resource planning at various levels.

Different people in the same teams have different thinking and working pattern. The difference increases more when it comes to different departments and their heads. The challenge increases manifold if the interaction has to be between the members of varied teams. Here comes the role of coordination. Coordination is the act of coordinating, and making different people or things work together for a goal or effect. Obviously, a manager has to be adept in the art of coordination.

Human resource management can be defined as a collection of those managerial activities that are associated with human resources planning, recruitment, selection, orientation, training, appraisal, motivation, remuneration, etc. HRM aims at developing people through work

Edwin B. Flippo defined HRM as "planning, organizing, directing, controlling of procurement, development, compensation, integration, maintenance, and separation of human resources to the end that individual, organizational and social objectives are achieved."

According to French Wendell- "Personnel management is a major component of the broader managerial function and has roots and branches extending throughout and beyond each organization. It is a major sub-system of all organizations."

According to Gary Dessler – "Human Resource Management is the process of acquiring, training, appraising, and compensating employees, and attending to their labour relations, health, safety and fairness concerns."

Objectives of human resource management

- To help the organization reach its goals.
- To ensure effective utilization and maximum development of human resources.
- To ensure respect for human beings to identify and satisfy the needs of individuals.
- To ensure reconciliation of individual goals with those of the organization.
- To achieve and maintain high morale among employees.
- To provide the organization with well-trained and well-motivated employees.
- To increase to the fullest the employee's job satisfaction and self-actualization.
- To develop and maintain a quality of work life.
- To be ethically and socially responsive to the needs of society.
- To develop the overall personality of each employee in its multidimensional aspect.
- To enhance employees' capabilities to perform the present job.

The objectives of HRM can be broken down into four broad categories:

Societal objectives: Measures put into place that responds to the ethical and social needs or challenges of the company and its employees. This includes legal issues such as equal opportunity and equal pay for equal work.

Organizational objectives: Actions are taken that help to ensure the efficiency of the organization. This includes providing training, hiring the right number of employees for a given task, or maintaining high employee retention rates.

Functional objectives: Guidelines used to keep HR functioning properly within the organization as a whole. This includes making sure that all of HR's resources are being allocated to their full potential.

Personal objectives: Resources used to support the personal goals of each employee. This includes offering the opportunity for education or career development as well as maintaining employee satisfaction.

Personnel Management vs. Human Resource Management

1. Personnel management is a traditional approach to managing people in the organization. Human resource management is a modern approach to managing people and their strengths in the organization.

2. Personnel management focuses on personnel administration, employee welfare, and labor relation. Human resource management focuses on the acquisition, development, motivation, and maintenance of human resources in the organization.

3. Personnel management assumes people as input for achieving the desired output. Human resource management assumes people as an important and valuable resource for achieving the desired output.

4. Under personnel management, personnel function is undertaken for employee satisfaction. Under human resource management, the administrative function is undertaken for goal achievement.

5. Under personnel management, job design is done on the basis of the division of labor. Under human resource management, the job design function is done on the basis of group work/teamwork.

Human Resource Planning (HRP)

Human resource planning (HRP) or Manpower Planning is the continuous process of systematic planning ahead to achieve optimum use of an organization's most valuable asset—quality employees. Human resource planning ensures the best fit between employees and jobs while avoiding manpower shortages or surpluses.

According to E.W. Vetter, human resource planning is "the process by which a management determines how an organization should make from its current manpower position to its desired manpower position".

Dale S. Beach has defined it as "a process of determining and assuring that the organization will have an adequate number of qualified persons available at the proper times, performing jobs which meet the needs of the enterprise and which provide satisfaction for the individuals involved."

Steps in Manpower Planning

1. *Analyzing the current manpower inventory*-Before a manager makes a forecast of future manpower, the current manpower status has to be analyzed. For this, the following things have to be noted-

- Type of organization
- Number of departments
- Number and quantity of such departments

Employees in these work units Once these factors are registered by a manager, he goes for the future forecasting.

2. *Making future manpower forecasts-* Once the factors affecting the future manpower forecasts are known, planning can be done for the future manpower requirements in several work units. The Manpower forecasting techniques commonly employed by the organizations are as follows:

Expert Forecasts: This includes informal decisions, formal expert surveys, and the Delphi technique.

Trend Analysis: Manpower needs can be projected through extrapolation (projecting past trends), indexation (using base year as a basis), and statistical analysis (central tendency measure).

Work Load Analysis: It is dependent upon the nature of workload in a department, a branch, or division.

Work Force Analysis: Whenever production and time period has to be analyzed, due allowances have to be made for getting net manpower requirements.

Other methods: Several Mathematical models, with the aid of computers, are used to forecast manpower needs, like budget and planning analysis, regression, and new venture analysis.

3. *Developing employment programs-* Once the current inventory is compared with future forecasts, the employment programs can be framed and developed accordingly, which will include recruitment, selection procedures, and placement plans.

4. *Design training programs-* These will be based upon the extent of diversification, expansion plans, development programs, etc. Training programs depend upon the extent of improvement in technology and advancement to take place. It is also done to improve upon the skills, capabilities, and knowledge of the workers.

Recruitment

Recruitment is the process of actively seeking out, finding, and hiring candidates for a specific position or job. Recruitment is the process of locating and encouraging potential applicants to apply for existing or anticipated job openings. It is actually a linking function, joining together those with jobs to fill and those seeking jobs. Recruitment, logically, aims at

(i) attracting a large number of qualified applicants who are ready to take up the job if it's offered and

(ii) offering enough information for unqualified persons to self-select themselves out

Recruitment is a positive process of searching for prospective employees and stimulating them to apply for jobs in the organisation. When more people apply for jobs then there will be scope for recruiting better people. Recruitment is concerned with reaching out, attracting, and ensuring a supply of qualified personnel and making out a selection of requisite manpower both in their quantitative and qualitative aspect. It is the development and maintenance of adequate manpower resources.

According to Edwin B. Flippo, "It is a process of searching for prospective employees and stimulating and encouraging them to apply for jobs in an organisation." He further elaborates it, terming it both negative and positive.

In the words of Dale Yoder, Recruitment is the process of "discover the sources of manpower to meet the requirements of the staffing schedule and to employ effective measures for attracting that manpower in adequate numbers to facilitate effective selection of an efficient working force."

Kempner writes, "Recruitment forms the first stage in the process which continues with selection and ceases with the placement of the candidates."

Sources of Recruitment of Employees

Searching for suitable candidates and informing them about the openings in the enterprise is the most important aspect of the recruitment process. The candidates may be available inside or outside the organisation. Basically, there are two sources of recruitment i.e., internal and external sources

(A) Internal Sources: Best employees can be found within the organization when a vacancy arises in the organisation, it may be given to an employee who is already on the payroll. Internal sources include a promotion, transfer, and in certain cases demotion. When a higher post is given to a deserving employee, it motivates all other employees of the organisation to work hard. The employees can be informed of such a vacancy by internal advertisement.

The Internal Sources are :

1. Transfers: Transfer involves shifting of persons from present jobs to other similar jobs. These do not involve any change in rank, responsibility, or prestige. The number of persons does not increase with transfers.

2. Promotions: Promotions refer to the shifting of persons to positions carrying better prestige, higher responsibilities, and more pay. The higher

positions falling vacant may be filled up from within the organisation. Promotion does not increase the number of persons in the organisation. A person going to get a higher position will vacate his present position. Promotion will motivate employees to improve their performance so that they can also get promotions.

3. Present Employees: The present employees of concern are informed about likely vacant positions. The employees recommend their relations or persons intimately known to them. Management is relieved of looking out for prospective candidates. The persons recommended by the employees may be generally suitable for the jobs because they know the requirements of various positions. The existing employees take full responsibility for those recommended by them and also ensure their proper behaviour and performance.

(B) External Sources: All organisations have to use external sources for recruitment to higher positions when existing employees are not suitable. More persons are needed when expansions are undertaken. The external sources are discussed below:

1. Advertisement: It is a method of recruitment frequently used for skilled workers, clerical and higher staff. Advertisements can be given in newspapers and professional journals. These advertisements attract applicants in a large number of highly variable quality. Preparing a good advertisement is a specialized task. If a company wants to conceal its name, a 'blind advertisement' may be given asking the applicants to apply to Post Bag or Box Number or to some advertising agency.

2. Employment Exchanges: Employment exchanges in India are run by the Government. For unskilled, semi-skilled, skilled, clerical posts, etc., it is often used as a source of recruitment. In certain cases, it has been made obligatory for the business concerns to notify their vacancies to the employment exchange. In the past, employers used to turn to these agencies only as a last resort. Job- seekers and job-givers are brought into contact by the employment exchanges.

3. Schools, Colleges, and Universities: Direct recruitment from educational institutions for certain jobs (i.e. placement) which require technical or professional qualifications has become a common practice. A close liaison between the company and educational institutions helps in getting suitable candidates. The students are spotted during the course of their studies. Junior-level executives or managerial trainees may be recruited in this way.

4. **Recommendation of Existing Employees:** The present employees know both the company and the candidate recommended. Hence some companies encourage their existing employees to assist them in getting applications from persons who are known to them. In certain cases, rewards may also be given if candidates recommended by them are actually selected by the company. If recommendation leads to favoritism, it will impair the morale of employees.

5. **Factory Gates:** Certain workers present themselves at the factory gate every day for employment. This method of recruitment is very popular in India for unskilled or semi-skilled labour. The desirable candidates are selected by the first-line supervisors. The major disadvantage of this system is that the person selected may not be suitable for the vacancy.

6. **Casual Callers:** That personnel who casually come to the company for employment may also be considered for the vacant post. It is the most economical method of recruitment. In advanced countries, this method of recruitment is very popular.

7. **Former Employees:** In case employees have been laid off or have left the factory on their own, they may be taken back if they are interested in joining the concern (provided their record is good).

8. **Labour Unions:** In certain occupations like construction, hotels, etc., all recruits usually come from unions. It is advantageous from the management's point of view because it saves the expenses of recruitment. However, in other industries, unions may be asked to recommend candidates either as a goodwill gesture or as a courtesy to the union.

9. **Labour Contractors:** This method of recruitment is still prevalent in India for hiring unskilled and semi-skilled workers. The contractors keep themselves in touch with the labour and bring the workers to the places where they are required. They get a commission for the number of persons supplied by them.

Methods of recruitment

The following recruitment methods are approaches that companies might consider when they are searching for the best recruitment methods.

1. Employee Referral Programs

Employee referrals are among some of the best recruitment strategies for businesses. Existing employees know the company culture and usually, only refer candidates they consider to be a cultural fit. When employees are included in the recruitment process, they can share vacancies with people in their networks.

2. Internships

Companies that offer internships have the opportunity to learn the strengths of individual interns. An internship can be used as a long-term interview process. During the internship, HR professionals can evaluate the interns and identify people who might be tapped to fill future vacancies.

3. Word-of-Mouth

A word-of-mouth recruitment strategy is more suitable for large brands for applicants applying to them every day. These employers have established brands and are considered to be choice employers. These types of companies only have to let people know that they are hiring, and they will have plenty of applicants for their vacancies.

4. Recruitment Events

Networking recruitment events can be a good way for companies that are planning to expand to attract suitable candidates. An event can include participating in job fairs, offering recruitment drives on college campuses, or hosting open days. However, participating in recruitment events can be expensive. Before deciding to participate in a recruitment event, the company should understand the specific qualities and skill-sets that they are looking for in candidates.

5. Social Media

Companies should include using social media in their recruitment efforts. Many people who are looking for jobs use social media as a part of their job search. Since so many applicants search for jobs on social media channels, it makes sense for companies to go where the talent pool is.

Recruitment process

Recruitment Process can be defined as "it is a way to attract and find potential manpower to fill up the vacant post in the company". The HR Recruitment Process helps to hire candidates based on their ability to work and attitude which is essential for accomplishment of organizational goals.

1. Recruitment Planning
2. Strategy development
3. Searching
4. Screening
5. Evaluation and control

Selection

Selection is the process of carefully screening the candidates who offer themselves for the appointment so as to choose the most suitable persons for the jobs that are to be filled. It is the process of matching the qualifications of candidates with the requirements of jobs to be filled.

In the words of Dale Yoder, "Selection is the process by which candidates are divided into two classes-those who will be offered employment and those who will not?"

According to O.Donnell, "Selection is the process of choosing from among the candidates, from within the organization or from the outside, the most suitable person for the current position or for the future position."

Selection process

The procedure of selection will vary from organisation to organisation and even from department to department within the same organisation according to the kinds of the jobs to be filled. The number of steps in the procedure and the sequence of steps also varies.Every organisation will design a selection procedure that suits its requirements. However, the main steps or stages that could be incorporated in the selection procedure are as under:

1. Preliminary interview
2. Receiving applications
3. Screening of applications
4. Employment tests
5. Employment interview
6. Checking references
7. Medical examination
8. Final selection

Stage 1: Preliminary Interview

In most organisations, the selection program begins with a preliminary interview or screening. The preliminary interview is generally brief and does the job of eliminating the totally unsuitable candidates. The preliminary interview offers advantages not only to the organisation, but also to the applicants. If an applicant is eliminated at this stage, the organisation will be saved from the expenses of processing him through the remaining steps of the selection procedure and the unsuitable candidate will be saved from the trouble of passing through the long procedure. Preliminary interviews may take place across the counter in the organisations employment office. It may consist of a short exchange of information with respect to organisation's interest in hiring and the candidate's enquiry. It may serve primarily to determine whether it is worthwhile for the applicant to fill in the application blank. Candidates who pass this crucial screening are usually asked to fill in the application blank available with the employment office of the organisation

Stage 2: Receiving Applications

Whenever there is a vacancy it is advertised or enquiries are made from suitable sources, and applications are received from the candidates. Standard application forms may be drawn up for different jobs and supplied to the candidates on request. The application form is useful for several reasons. It gives a preliminary idea of the candidate to the interviewer and helps him in formulating questions to have more information about the candidate. The written information about age qualifications, experience, etc. may prove to be of greater value to the interviewers. It makes the processing of applications very easy since there is uniformity in filling the data in the application form

Stage 3: Screening of Applications

After the applications are received, they are screened by a screening committee and a list is prepared of the candidates to be interviewed. Applicants may be called for interviews on some specific criteria like sex, desired age group experience, and qualifications. The number of candidates to be called for an interview is normally five to seven times the number of posts to the filled up. The screened applications are then reviewed by the Personnel Manager and interview letters are despatched by registered post or under certificate of a post.

Stage 4: Employment Tests

Individuals differ in almost all aspects one can think of. They differ with respect to physical characteristics, capacity level of mental ability likes and dislikes, and also with respect to personality traits. The pattern of physical, mental, and personal variables gives rise to thousand and one combinations and the particular pattern makes the individual suitable for several classes of activities. jobs or fields of work. Matching of individual's physical, mental and temperamental pattern with the requirements of a job or field of training is a difficult task. But where this matching takes place, the result is happiness for the individual and prosperity for the organisation and the society. But instances of round pegs in square holes and vice versa are not rare. So before deciding upon the job or jobs suitable for a particular individual, one should know the level of his ability and the knowledge of the pattern of his interest and aptitudes in detail. This will require the use of employment tests which are listed below:

(i) Intelligence tests.

(ii) Aptitude tests.

(iii) Trade or proficiency tests

(iv) Interest tests

(v) Personality tests.

Employment tests are widely used for judging the applicant's suitability for the job. They bring out the qualities and weaknesses of individuals which could be analysed before offering them jobs. The tests must be designed properly. If they are biased, they will not be good indicators of one's knowledge and skills. Selections based on such tests will be faulty. That is why tests should not be relied upon fully.

Stage 5: Employment Interview

Although application blank and employment tests provide a lot of valuable information about the candidate, they do not provide the complete information required of the applicant. An interview may be used to secure more information about the candidate. The main purposes of an employment interview are: (a) to find out the suitability of the candidate, (b) to seek more information about the candidate, and (c) to give him an accurate picture of the job with details of terms and conditions and some idea of organisation's policies

For the selection of the right types of people, an employment interview is very important. The communication skill of the candidate can be judged in the interview, His way of thinking can also be known. An interview is very important where the candidate has not to go through employment tests. The information contained in the application blank can be checked during the interview.

The factual data of the applicant given in the application form may be checked and more information may be obtained from the candidate. This occasion is also utilised for testing the capability and personality of the applicant. Thus, an interview affords an opportunity to develop a clear picture of the candidate. It is customary to have an interview in several stages, especially for senior positions. There may be a preliminary interview by the head of the department. The final interview is taken by the Interview or Selection Committee consisting of the chairman of the organisation, head of the department, human resource manager, and outside experts. During the interview, the members of the selection committee appraise each candidate according to merit. At the end of the interview of each candidate, the chairman consults the members and after a brief discussion finalises the grading of the candidate. After all the candidates have been interviewed, a panel is prepared. The number of persons in the panel is generally about two to three times the number of vacancies to be filled up.

Stage 6: Checking References

A referee is potentially an important source of information about a candidate's ability and personality if he holds a responsible position in some organisation or has been the boss or employer of the candidate. Prior to the final selection, the prospective employer normally makes an investigation of the references supplied by the applicant and undertakes more or less a thorough search into the candidate's past employment, education, personal reputation, financial condition, police record, etc. However, it is often difficult to persuade a referee to give his opinion frankly. The organisation may persuade him to do so by giving an assurance that all information provided by him will be treated as strictly confidential.

Stage 7: Medical Examination

A pre-employment physical examination or medical test of a candidate is an important step in the selection procedure. Though in the suggested selection procedure, the medical test is located near the end, this sequence need not be rigid. The organisations may place the medical examination relatively early in the process so as to avoid time and expenditure to be incurred on the selection of medically unfit persons. Some organisations either place the examination relatively early in the selection procedure or advise the candidates to get themselves examined by a medical expert so as to avoid disappointment at the end.

The physical examination should disclose the physical characteristics of the individual that are significant from the standpoint of his efficient performance of the job he may be assigned or of those jobs to which he may reasonably be expected to be transferred or promoted. A proper medical examination will ensure a higher standard of health and physical fitness for the employees and will reduce the rates of accidents, labour turnover, and absenteeism.

Stage 8: Final Selection and Appointment Letter

After a candidate has cleared all the hurdles in the selection procedure, he is formally appointed by issuing him an appointment letter or by concluding with him a service agreement. Generally, the candidates are not appointed on a permanent basis because it is considered better to try them for a few months on the job itself. This is because no procedure of selection is complete in itself to find out the whole picture of the personality and qualities of a candidate. It is only by observing a person at work that one can find out how he does his work and behaves with fellow employees and supervisors. If during the probation period, an employee is found unsuitable, the management may transfer him to some other job to which he may be expected to do justice. But if the organisation cannot offer him a job that he can do well, the management may either sack him or give him time and training to improve himself.

TRAINING

Training is an organised activity for increasing the knowledge and skills of people for a definite purpose. It involves systematic procedures for transferring technical know-how to the employees so as to increase their knowledge and skills for doing specific jobs with proficiency. In other words, the trainees acquire technical knowledge, skills, and problem-solving ability by undergoing the training program. It refers to a program that facilitates an employee to perform the job effectively through acquiring increased knowledge and skills. According to Edwin B Flippo," Training is the act of increasing the knowledge and skills of an employee for doing a particular job."

The objectives of the training are as follows:

(i) To increase the knowledge of workers in doing specific jobs.

(ii) To impart new skills among the workers systematically so that they learn quickly.

(iii) To bring about change in the attitudes of the workers towards fellow workers, supervisors, and the organisation.

(iv) To improve the overall performance of the organisation.

(v) To make the workers handle materials, machines, and equipment efficiently and thus to check wastage of time and resources.

(vi) To reduce the number of accidents by providing safety training to workers.

(vii) To prepare workers for higher jobs by developing advanced skills in them.

Types of Training

On the basis of purpose, several types of training programs are offered to the employees. It should be noted that these programs are not mutually exclusive. They invariably overlap and employ many common techniques. The important types of training programs are as follows:

1. Induction or orientation training.

2. Job training.

3. Apprenticeship training

4. Internship training

5. Refresher training or retraining.

6. Training for promotion.

1. Induction or Orientation Training

Induction is concerned with introducing or orienting a new employee to the organisation and its procedures, rules, and regulations. When a new employee reports for work, he must be helped to get acquainted with the work environment and fellow employees. It is better to give him a friendly welcome when he joins the organisation, get him introduced to the organisation and help him to get a general idea about the rules and regulations, working conditions, etc. of the organisation.

Employee orientation or induction training is nothing but the introduction of the organisation to the newly employed person. The purpose is to give a 'bird's eye view of the organisation where he has to work. It is a very short informative training given immediately after recruitment. It creates a feeling of involvement in the minds of newly appointed employees.

2 Job Training

Job training relates to a specific job that the worker has to handle. It gives information about machines, the process of production, instructions to be followed, methods to be used, and so on. It develops skills and confidence among the workers and enables them to perform the job efficiently.

Job training is the most common of formal in-plant training programs. It is necessary for the new employees to acquaint themselves with the jobs they are expected to perform. It helps in creating the interest of the employees in their jobs.

3. Apprenticeship Training

Apprenticeship training program tends more toward education than merely vocational training. Under this, both knowledge and skills in doing a job or a series of related jobs are involved. The governments of various countries have passed laws that make it obligatory for certain classes of employers to provide apprenticeship training to young people. The usual apprenticeship programs combine on-the-job training and experience with classroom instructions in particular subjects.

The trainees receive wages while learning and they acquire valuable skills which command a high wage in the labour market. In India, there are so many 'earn then you learn' schemes both in the private as well as public sector undertakings. This is also advantageous to the trainees. Some employers look upon apprentices as a source of cheap labour. Apprenticeship training is desirable in industries that require a constant flow of new employees expected to become all-around craftsmen. It is very much prevalent in printing trades, building and construction, and crafts like mechanics, electricians, welders, etc.

4. Internship Training

Under this method, the educational or vocational institute enters into an arrangement with an industrial enterprise for providing practical knowledge to its students. Internship training is usually meant for such vocations where advanced theoretical knowledge is to be backed up by practical experience on the job. For instance, engineering students are sent to big industrial enterprises for gaining practical work experience and medical students are sent to big hospitals to get practical knowledge. The period of such training varies from six months to two years. The trainees do not belong to business enterprises, but they come from vocational or professional institutions. It is quite usual that enterprises giving them training absorb them by offering suitable jobs.

5. Refresher Training or Retraining

As the name implies, the refresher training is meant for the old employees of the enterprise. The basic purpose of the refresher training is to acquaint the existing workforce with the latest methods of performing their jobs and improve their efficiency further. In the words of Dale Yoder, "Retraining programs are designed to avoid personnel obsolescence." The skills of the existing employees become obsolete because of technological changes and because of the tendency of human beings to forget. Thus, refresher training is essential because of the following factors:

(a) The workers require training to bring them up-to-date with the knowledge and skills and to relearn what they have forgotten.

(b) Rapid technological changes make even qualified workers obsolete in course of time because new technology is associated with new work methods and job requirements. The workers need to learn new work methods to use new techniques in doing their jobs.

(c) Refresher training becomes necessary because many new jobs which are created due to changes in the demand for goods and services are to be handled by the existing employees.

6. Training for Promotion

The talented employees may be given adequate training to make them eligible for promotion to higher jobs in the organisation Promotion of an employee means a significant change in his responsibilities and duties. Therefore, it is essential that he is provided sufficient training to learn new skills to perform his new duties efficiently. The purpose of training for promotion is to develop the existing employees to make them fit for undertaking higher job responsibilities. This serves as a motivating force for the employees.

METHODS OF TRAINING

A wide range of training methods and techniques have been developed over the years by various organisations and training experts. Different training methods are suitable for different categories of personnel in the organisation: managerial and non-managerial, technical, administrative, skilled, unskilled, senior, junior, and so on. Each organisation has to choose those methods and techniques of training which are relevant to its training needs.

The various methods of training may be classified into the following categories:

1. On-the-job training

II. Vestibule training

III. Off-the-job training

Methods of Training

L. On-the-job Training (at the place of work)

(i) Coaching

(ii) Understudy

(iii) Position Rotation.

II. Vestibule Training (adapted to the environment at the place of work)

III. Off-the-job Training (away from the place of work)

(i) Classroom training

(ii) Conference

(iii) Case Study

(iv) Sensitivity training

(v) Special projects

(vi) Committee assignments.

On-the-job training

On-the-job training is considered to be the most effective method of training the operative personnel. Under this method, the worker is given training at the workplace by his immediate supervisor. In other words, the worker learns in the actual work environment. It is based on the principle of learning by doing. On-the-job training techniques are most appropriate for imparting knowledge and skills that can be learned in a relatively short period of time and where only a few employees are to be trained at a time. But the success of the training depends almost entirely on the trainer. If he understands training principles and methods and if he takes an interest in the proper training of new employees, chances are that the employees will be trained properly.

There are three methods of on-the-job training described below:

(i) Coaching- Under this method, the supervisor imparts job knowledge and skills to his subordinate. The emphasis in coaching or instructing the subordinate is on learning by doing. This method is very effective if the superior has sufficient time to provide coaching to his subordinates.

(ii) Understudy- The superior gives training to a subordinate as his understudy or assistant. The subordinate learns through experience and observation. It prepares the subordinate to assume the responsibilities of the superior's job in case the superior leaves the organisation.

The subordinate chosen for under-study is designated as the heir-apparent and his future depends upon what happens to his boss. The purpose of under study is to prepare someone to fill the vacancy caused by death or retirement. promotion, or transfer of the superior.

(iii) Position Rotation-The purpose of position rotation is to broaden the background of the trainee in various positions. The trainee is periodically rotated from job to job instead of sticking to one job so that he acquires a general background of different jobs. However, the rotation of an employee from one job to another should not be done frequently. He should be allowed to stay on a job for a sufficient period so that he may acquire the full knowledge of the job.

Job rotation is used by many organisations to develop all-around workers. The employees learn new skills and gain experience in handling different kinds of jobs. They also come to know the interrelationship between different jobs. Job rotation is also used to place workers in the right jobs and prepare them to handle other jobs in case of need.

Vestibule training

The term 'vestibule training' is used to designate training in a classroom for semi-skilled jobs. It is more suitable where a large number of employees must be trained at the same time for the same kind of work. Where this method is used, there should be well-qualified instructors in charge of the training program. Here the emphasis tends to be on learning rather than production. It is frequently used to train clerks, machine operators, typists, etc.

Vestibule training is adapted to the general type of training problem that is faced by on-the-job training. An attempt is made to duplicate, as nearly as possible, the materials, equipment, and conditions found in the real workplace.

The human resource department makes arrangements for vestibule training when the training work exceeds the capacity of the line supervisors. Thus, in vestibule training, the workers are trained on specific jobs as they would be expected to perform at their workplace. An attempt is made to create working conditions that are similar to the actual workshop conditions. The learning takes place under the guidance of expert trainees.

Vestibule training is particularly suitable where it is not advisable to put the burden of training on line supervisors and where a special kind of learning is required. The trainers include expert and specialist instructors. The trainees avoid the confusion and pressure of the workplace and are thus able to concentrate on training. Their activities do not interfere with the regular processes of production. Moreover, the trainees get an opportunity to become accustomed to the work routine and recover from their initial nervousness before going on to their workplace.

Off-the-job training

It requires the worker to undergo training for a specific period away from the work-place. Off-the-job methods are concerned with both knowledge and skills in doing certain jobs. The workers are free of the tension of work when they are learning. There are several off-the-job methods of training and development as described below:

(i) Classroom Training (Lecture Method)-Classroom training is more associated with imparting knowledge than with skills. The special lectures may be delivered by some executives of the organisation or specialists from vocational and professional institutes.

(ii) Conference Training- A conference is a group meeting conducted according to an organised plan in which the members seek to develop knowledge and understanding by oral participation. It is an effective training device for persons in the positions of both conference member and conference leader. As a member, a person can learn from others by comparing his opinions with those of others. He learns to respect the viewpoints of others and also realises that there is more than one workable approach to any problem.

The literal meaning of conference is 'consultation. But in practice, a conference implies sharing some information with an audience of a large number of people. It is conducted in a big hall where the participants are allowed to exchange their views and raise queries. The proceedings of the conference are conducted by the chairman who is also responsible for summing up the proceedings of the conference.

(iii) Role playing-This technique is used for human relations and leadership training. Its purpose is to increase the trainee's skills in dealing with others. Under this method, two trainees are assigned different roles to play. For instance, one may play the role of a Sales Executive and the other that of a Customer. Both will interact with each other and play their respective roles. This will help the trainees in learning how to behave in a conflict situation. They will also learn to appreciate the viewpoints of each other.

(iv)Case Study-The case study method is a means of simulating experience in the classroom. Under this method, the trainees are given a problem or case which is more or less related to the concepts and principles already taught. They analyse the problem and suggest solutions that are discussed in the class. The instructor helps them reach a common solution to the problem. This method gives the trainee an opportunity to apply his knowledge to the solution of realistic problems.

Cases may be used in either of the two ways. Firstly, they can be used subsequent to the expansion of formal theory under which the trainees apply their knowledge of theory to specific situations. Secondly, the trainees may be assigned the cases for written analysis and oral discussion in the class without any prior explanation of pertinent concepts and theory. The case study places heavy demands upon the trainees and requires that they should have a good deal of maturity in the subject matter concerned.

Off-the-job methods are more relevant for the development of higher-level employees and executives. In addition to the above methods, sensitivity training, seminars, special projects, and committee assignments may also be used for the training and development of employees.

CHAPTER VII

PERFORMANCE APPRAISAL

A performance appraisal used in the organization is a regular review of employees' performance to verify their contribution to the company. It is also known as an annual review or performance evaluation. It evaluates the skills, growth, achievement, or failure of the employees. The performance appraisal is often used to justify the decisions related to promotions, pay hikes, bonuses, and termination of employees. Performance Appraisal is the systematic evaluation of the performance of employees and understanding of the abilities of a person for further growth and development.

The term performance appraisal refers to the regular review of an employee's job performance and overall contribution to a company. Also known as an annual review, performance review or evaluation, or employee appraisal, a performance appraisal evaluates an employee's skills, achievements, and growth, or lack thereof. It is the periodic assessment of an employee's job performance as measured by the competency expectations set out by the organization. The performance assessment often includes both the core competencies required by the organization and also the competencies specific to the employee's job.

Performance appraisal is defined as a process that systematically measures an employee's personality and performance usually by managers or immediate supervisors against predefined attributes like skillset, knowledge about the role, technical know-how, attitude, punctuality, and so on.

Edwin B. Flippo defines Performance Appraisal as "a systematic, periodic and so far as humanly possible, an impartial rating of an employee's excellence in matters pertaining to his present job and his potentialities for a better job."

According to Dale Yoder, "Performance appraisal includes all formal procedures used to evaluate personalities and contributions and potentials of group members in a working organisation. It is a continuous process to secure information necessary for making correct and objective decisions on employees."

Objectives of Performance Appraisal

1. To maintain records to determine compensation packages, wage structure, salary raises, etc.
2. To identify the strengths and weaknesses of employees to place the right men on the right job.
3. To maintain and assess the potential present in a person for further growth and development.
4. To provide feedback to employees regarding their performance and related status.
5. To provide feedback to employees regarding their performance and related status.
6. It serves as a basis for influencing the working habits of the employees.
7. To review and retain the promotional and other training programs.

Purpose of Performance Appraisal

Appraisals serve different organizational and individual needs. The following are the reasons for carrying out a performance appraisal:

- to asses the employee's present level of performance
- to identify the strengths and weaknesses of individual employee
- to provide feedback to the employee so that he can improve his/her performance
- to provide an objective basis for rewarding the employees for their performance
- to motivate those employees who perform
- to check and facilitate those employees to perform who otherwise fail to perform
- to identify the gaps in performance, and thus, assess training and developmental needs
- to identify the employee's potential to perform
- to provide a database for evolving succession strategies
- to provide a basis for many other decisions such as fixation of incentives or increment, regularization or confirmation of the services of the employee, employee's promotion. transfer or demotion.

Functions of Performance Appraisal

The primary functions of performance appraisal are:

1. To identify and define the specific job criteria. Many organisations at the beginning of the year set key performance areas (KPS) or key result areas (KRAs) for employees based on mutual discussions.
2. To measure and compare the performance in terms of the defined job criteria, KRAs and KPAs are also designed so that they can help in measuring job performance in quantitative or qualitative terms.
3. 3. To develop and justify a reward system, relating rewards to employee performance.
4. To identify the strengths and weaknesses of employees and to decide on proper placement and promotion.
5. To develop suitable training and development programs for enriching the performance of the employees.
6. To plan for long-term manpower requirements and to decide upon the organisational development programs needed, duly identifying the change areas (for overall improvement of the organisation).
7. To identify motivational reinforcers, develop communication systems, and also to strengthen superior-subordinate relationships.

Advantages of Performance Appraisal

- It helps the supervisors to chalk out the promotion for performing employees and dismiss the inefficient workers.
- It helps the organization to decide the compensation of the employee. Also, based on the performance and the additional efforts put by the employee the extra benefits and allowances can be decided using records of performance appraisal.
- Special actions can be taken for the development of the employees. The performance appraisal system will highlight the weakness of the employee based on which the training program arrangement can be carried out by the organization.
- The performance appraisal further suggests the changes in the selection process which will help to hire better employees.
- A performance review is an effective way to communicate the status of the performance of the employee. It is a way to provide feedback about how the employees are doing on their job.
- The evaluation of the performance can act as a motivational tool. It provides a picture of the efficiency of the employee and motivates the individual to improve their performance.

Disadvantages of Performance Appraisal

- Performance appraisal depends on the factors used for the evaluation of the performance. The use of incorrect or irrelevant factors can lead to the failure of performance appraisal.
- The factors like attitude, abilities, and initiative are very vague and difficult to judge.
- Sometimes the managers who carry out the performance appraisal are not qualified enough to properly assess the abilities of the employees. Thus, it leads to irrelevant data collection and failure of performance appraisal.

Types of Employee Performance Appraisal in HRM

In most organizations supervisors are in charge of performance appraisal. However, there are different types of employee performance appraisal in HRM based on the people who evaluate the performance of the employee.

The four major types of performance appraisal are as follows-

- Self-assessment: Here the employee rate their job performance and work behavior
- Peer assessment: Under this assessment, the team members, co-workers, and workgroup are responsible for the performance rating of the employee.
- 360-degree performance appraisal: In this type of appraisal the performance rating is collected from an employee, their immediate supervisor, and peers.
- Negotiated appraisal: To avoid conflicts between employee and their supervisors a new trend of appraisal is utilized. In this type of performance appraisal, a mediator evaluates the performance of the employee and puts focus on the good side of performance rather than the criticism.

Methods of performance appraisal

Performance means the degree or extent to which an employee applies his skill, knowledge, and efforts to a job, assigned to him and the result of that application. Performance appraisal means the analysis, review, or evaluation of the performance or behaviour analysis of an employee. It may be formal or informal, oral or documented, open or confidential. However, in organisations we find the formal appraisal system in a documented form. It is, therefore, a formal process to evaluate the performance of the employees in terms of achieving organisational objectives.

Different methods of performance appraisal are followed in different organisations to achieve the above objectives. Since some methods of performance appraisal are complicated and call for adequate knowledge of quantitative techniques, many organisations follow traditional methods of appraisal. In contrast, others consider modern methods as the basis for evaluating the job performance of their employees.

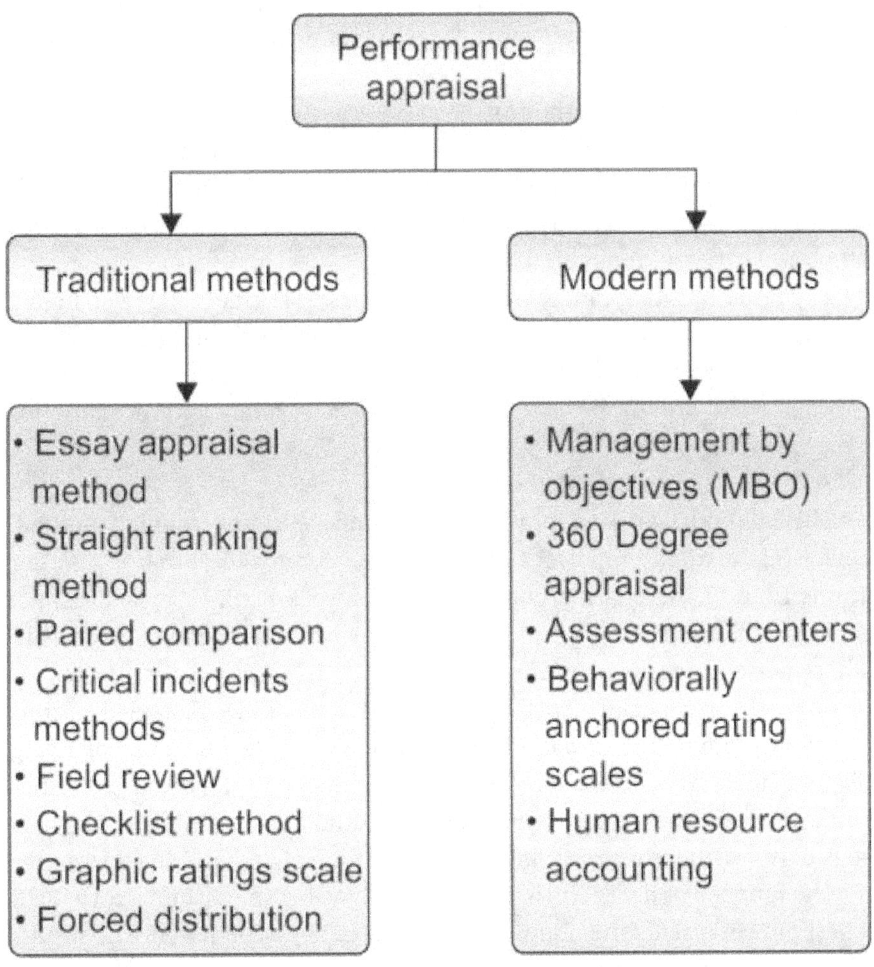

A. Traditional Methods:

These are the old methods of performance appraisal based on personal qualities like knowledge, capacity, judgment, initiative, attitude, loyalty, leadership, judgment, etc.

The following are the traditional methods of performance appraisal:

1. Unstructured Method of Appraisal:

This is a simple method of performance appraisal. It is highly subjective. Under this method, the appraiser has to describe his impressions of the employee under appraisal in an unstructured manner. Sometimes rater has to list his comments specifically on qualities, abilities, attitude, aptitude, and other personal traits of the employees. This makes the method highly subjective. Personal bias reflects through the impressions of the rater in his report.

2. Straight Ranking Method:

It is a quite simple and old method of performance appraisal. Under this method, the employee and his performance are considered as an entity. All the employees are evaluated by the appraiser considering their performance of job as a base and ranks are given.

The order of rating ranges from best to worst. This method is also highly subjective and lacks fairness in assessing the real worth of an employee. It becomes a difficult task when the performances of a pretty large number of employees are to be assessed. It lacks a systematic procedure for performance appraisal.

3. Paired Comparison Method:

This method is an attempt to improve upon the simple ranking method. Under this method employees of a group are compared with one another at one time. If there is a group of five employees A, B, C, D, and E then A's performance is compared with that of B's, and a decision is taken as to whose performance is better.

Similarly, A's performance is compared with C, D, E, and decisions regarding comparatively better performances are taken. The following diagram illustrates this fact. The same technique is followed for other employees. Under this paired comparison method ten decisions are arrived at as only two employees are involved at the time of arriving at a decision.

The number of decisions is determined by using the formula, n (n-1)/2 where "n" represents the number of employees to be compared. The results are tabulated and every employee is ranked. The paired comparison method is more reliable but the method is not suitable when large numbers of employees are to be evaluated.

4. Man to Man Comparison Method:

This method was used during World War I by the American army. Under this method, certain factors are selected for analysis. The factors include leadership qualities, initiative, etc. The appraiser develops a scale for each factor. Personnel is compared to key men as regards one factor at a time. This method is also known as the factor comparison method. The defect of this method is that developing a scale is quite a tough and complicated task.

5. Grading Method:

Under this technique of performance evaluation, certain categories of worth are determined in advance and they are carefully defined. These selected and well-defined categories include grades 'A' for outstanding, 'B' for very good, 'C' for average, 'D' for poor, etc. These grades are based on certain selected features of employees such as knowledge, judgment, analytical ability, leadership qualities, self-expression, etc. The actual performance of employees is compared with the above grades and employees are allotted grades that speak for their performance.

6. Graphic Rating Scale:

This is one of the most widely used performance evaluation techniques. The evaluator is asked to rate employees based on job-related characteristics and knowledge of the job. These can broadly be grouped as employee characteristics and employee contribution.

The evaluator is given printed forms. The employee characteristics include leadership qualities, initiative, industriousness attitude, cooperation, interest, creativity, loyalty, decision-making ability, analytical ability, dependability, etc. The employee contribution includes responsibility, quality of work, achievement of targets, versatility, relations with fellow employees and superiors, etc. The performance is evaluated based on these traits on a continuous scale.

Competence	Unacceptable 0	Weak 1	Fair 2	Good 3	Excellent 4
Reflection on relationship of specific teaching practices to student learning					
Establishment of inclusive learning environment					
Use of formative and summative assessments of learning					

Graphic Rating Scale

It is a standardized, quantitative method of performance appraisal. It is simple to understand and use. The scores are tabulated indicating the relative worth of each employee. This method has certain demerits. It is arbitrary and highly subjective. It assumes all characteristics are of equal importance for the performance of all jobs. It is charged that a high score on one factor may compensate low score on another. A supervisor may favour his subordinates unnecessarily. The evaluation cluster is on the high side.

7. Forced Choice Method:

This method was developed during World War II for evaluating the performance of American army personnel. The evaluators tend to rate the performance as high, moderate, or low and escape the important responsibility assigned to them. This method requires a more objective and least subjective assessment of the performance.

The rating elements are predetermined statements divided equally into negative and positive relating to efficiency and personal traits. The rationale is the statements are grouped having equal importance. The evaluator is forced to select from each group of statements (normally two).

The statements may be the following:

- Good work organizer.
- Shows patience with slow learners.
- Dishonest or disloyal.
- Careful and regular.
- Avoid work.
- Hard-working.

- Cooperates with fellow workers.
- Do not take interest in work.

From the above list of statements, favorable statements are marked plus and unfavorable statements are marked zero. Under this method subjectivity of the evaluator is eliminated if not completely.

8. Check List:

It is the simplest form of evaluation method. Under this method, a list of Statements describing the job-related behaviour of the employees is given to the evaluator. If the evaluator perceives that the employee possesses a particular trait, the statement is checked i.e. ticked and if he feels that the employee does not possess that quality he leaves it blank. He then submits it to the human resource department where counting of the checks is carried out and performance is assessed.

Weighted Checklist: The checklist provided to the evaluator contained statements relating to work-related behaviour and asked to check them if found within the employees. In this list weightage to the items is not given. Under the weighted checklist, the items having significant importance for organisational effectiveness are given weightage. The evaluator notes these checks and submits them to the authority for correct evaluation of the performance.

An example of the checklist is given below:

- Is the employee punctual?
- Is he interested in his job?
- Does he keep cool while working?
- Does he respect his superiors?
- Does he treat his subordinates well?
- Does he maintain machines in order?
- Does he follow orders without delay?

This method has some demerits. It suffers from the evaluator's bias. A separate checklist is required for each job which increases the cost. It is also difficult to provide due weightage to the particular characteristic of the employee.

9. Essay Method:

Under this method, no quantitative approach is undertaken. It is an open-ended appraisal of employees. Evaluator describes in his own words what he perceives about the employees' performance. He includes in his descriptions the knowledge, skill, interpersonal relations, temperament, quality and cost control aspects, needs for future development, etc. of the employees.

He tries his level best to describe the facts as correctly as possible. The report on the evaluation of performance is submitted in essay form. The supervisor can reveal more about the employee and while doing he cannot hide his weaknesses or strong points. This method is the most subjective. Some lack in ability to describe properly. An evaluator may favour his supporter with the best qualities even though the employee lacks in many aspects.

10. Critical Incidents Method:

Under this method, the performance of the worker is rated based on certain events that occur during the performance of the job i.e. the evaluation is based on key incidents. An emphasis is laid on the behaviour of the worker on the job. His behaviour is observed as to whether he becomes upset overwork, resists, cooperates with fellow workers, suggests an improvement in the method of work, etc. Various such behaviours are recorded by the supervisor.

The method requires that the behaviour of employees in all significant incidents be recorded the effective and ineffective behaviour in a specially designed notebook. The notebook contains various categories of characteristics of the employees.

An evaluator or supervisor here should refrain from passing his judgments but should discuss the facts as he observes. Like other methods, this method is also with limitations. A negative incident is more easily noticeable than the positive one to the supervisor. If the recording of the incident is put off for some time supervisor may forget the same and fails to record it later. It requires very close supervision which is generally not liked by the employees.

11. Field Review Method:

Under this method, a supervisor is interviewed by a human resource expert from the human resource department. The evaluator is equipped with test questions usually memorized by him which asks the supervisor. The supervisor is expected to give his opinion about the subordinates such as about his weakness and strength, outstanding ability, willingness to cooperate, etc. The evaluator records the details which are approved by the supervisor and these are kept in the personal file of the employee.

To make the method more effective evaluator must be well-versed and competent in his job. This method is useful for a large organisation where lots of employees are working. It is not suitable for small organisations.

B. Modern Methods

The traditional methods of performance appraisal discussed above, suffer from a major limitation for their obvious emphasis on assessing individual performance or task, considering it as an isolated factor. To eliminate such a narrow and partial approach, newer techniques of performance appraisal have been developed and are widely practiced by organisations, particularly for managerial and supervisory employees. Some of the modern techniques are discussed in the following subsections.

1. Management by Objectives (MBO)

In this method, managers and employees collaborate to identify, plan, organize, and communicate objectives. This is usually for a specific appraisal period and objectives are validated using the SMART (Specific, Measurable, Achievable, Realistic & Time-sensitive) method.

After setting clear goals, managers and employees interact periodically to discuss the feasibility of achieving set objectives and the progress made. These measures of progress help analyze the contributions of an employee at the end of the review period. Success is rewarded with appraisals like salary hikes or promotions, whereas others are re-evaluated for further training.

2. 360-Degree Feedback Method

The 360-degree appraisal involves the rating of an employee or manager by everyone an employee interacts with like managers, customers, peers, etc. When data is collected from multiple sources, the chances of a manager's bias affecting the appraisal are eliminated. Plus, it offers a clearer picture of the employee's competence in terms of work.

Components of 360 Degree Appraisal

The components of 360 degree appraisal are described as under:

Self Appraisal: Self-appraisal is a very important part of the 360 degree appraisal system because it gives the employee absolute freedom to look at his strengths and an opportunity to assess his performance. In a well established system, employees use the tool of self appraisal very effectively and organisations also find that employees often are their own strongest critics and display very high degree of objectivity. Self appraisal also provides an opportunity to the employee to express his career moves for the future.

Superior Appraisal: This is the most important aspect of the 360-degree appraisal system, but the emphasis here is on providing constructive feedback on an employee's performance and development needs. It is the superior's responsibility to ensure that employees set goals not only in terms of business performance but also in areas that are critical to the organisation. These are called corporate thrust areas and may include relationship management, safety, and quality development.

Peer Group Appraisal: Peers play an important role in the life of an employee in the organisation. They can also provide a deep insight into the personality makeup, attitude, and style of working of the employee. For better results, it is essential to select the right peers for the appraisal. They must include peers both from within the department as well as from the other departments which are directly connected with the working of the employee's department. Three to five internal customers should normally be chosen for peer appraisal.

Peer appraisal must strive to get feedback on (a) employee's working style, (b) sensitivity towards others, (c) spirit of co-operation and collaboration, and (d) ability to work as a team member

Subordinates' Appraisal: The most distinctive feature of 360-degree appraisal is the role of subordinates in appraisal. It signifies two things. Firstly, it is a clear expression from the organisation that it encourages openness and that feedback is a two-way process. Secondly, it is a systemic recognition of the fact that an employee's subordinates do play a vital role in his appraisal. Thus, the purpose of a subordinate appraisal is to get a first-hand assessment of how the subordinates perceive their superior to be in terms of

(a) delegation of authority, (b) guiding and training of subordinates, (c) motivation of subordinates, (d) team building, etc.

The upward appraisal also provides an opportunity for the subordinates to give feedback to their superiors about the kind of things they would like him/her to continue doing, and things they would like him/her to stop doing, things they would like him/her to start doing.

3. Assessment Center Method

Introduced by the German Army in the 1930s, the concept of the assessment center has been revamped to suit the current business scenario. The employees are assessed based on their performance through social-stimulating exercises like role-playing, decision-making, informal discussions, etc. The assessment evaluates the performance of employees to identify future leaders and managers.

The effectiveness of the Assessment Center Method allows employees to get a clear picture of their performance and how others observe them. The impact of others' perspectives on their performance can also be realized from these exercises. It is easier to evaluate the current performance of an employee and also predict future performance.

4. Human Resource Accounting Method

Also known as Human Resource Cost Accounting Method, it is used to evaluate an employee's performance as per the monetary benefits they yield from the organization. This means the performance of an employee is compared against the salary & other costs the company pays to the employee.

The cost of retaining an employee regarding their contribution is evaluated to get the cost of that employee for the organization. This method of performance appraisal considers factors like work quality, overhead cost, unit-wise average service value, interpersonal skills, and, so on. The idea is to analyze how the contributions compared with regard to cost (recruiting, hiring, training, and development) benefit the organization. In this method, the company appraises employees based on the cost to the company and the value they offer.

5. Behaviorally Anchored Rating Scale (BARS)

In this modern method of performance appraisal, both the qualitative and quantitative aspects of an employee are evaluated. BARS compare an employee's performance with specific behavioral examples that are assigned a numerical rating. As per the employee's role and job level, BARS has a set of predetermined standards called BARS statements. These statements are used as yardsticks to measure the performance on each BARS scale level.

BARS sets typical workplace behaviors as per a job role and evaluates an employee's performance in comparison to these set standards. How an employee should behave in any given situation (critical incidents) is measured as per the expected behavior. The performance appraisal with BARS provides more accurate and unbiased results.

6. Potential Appraisal

A potential appraisal is a holistic approach for studying the wholesome qualities of an employee with a given intellect, personality, and character. Industry practices apply two widely used approaches for potential appraisal, i.e., helicopter and whole person qualities. The helicopter method tries to measure the potentiality of a person on large as well as on specific issues. The whole person qualities method measures the wholesome qualities/ potentialities of a person with a given set of variables, mentioned above, which are already determined for the person. Potential appraisal data is extremely useful for career planning, as the latent abilities of an individual can be captured and matched with the future role and responsibilities. However, in India, we do not have documented practices on potential appraisal in the corporate world.

Steps in the Appraisal Process

1. Establish performance standards

Performance standards are set to ensure the achievement of departmental goals and objectives and the organization's overall strategy and objectives. Standards are based on the position, rather than an individual. To be clearly understood and perceived as objective, standards should adhere to the same rules that apply to goal-setting; that is, they should be "SMART:" specific, measurable, achievable, relevant, and time-bound.

2. Communicate performance standards

To be effective, performance standards must be communicated and understood to be expectations. Performance standards assume that an individual is competent, so initial and corrective training should be factored into the performance management process. If there is a specific training period after which an employee is assumed to be competent and performing to standards, that should be communicated as well.

3. Measure performance

Performance that is expressed in numeric terms—for example, cost, quantity, quality, timeliness—is relatively easy to measure. Performance in the area of soft skills—for example, communication, customer service, and leadership—is more difficult to evaluate. The focus should be on measuring what matters rather than measuring what's easy to measure.

4. Compare actual performance to performance standards

In this step of the appraisal process, actual performance is compared to the performance standards. Documentation should highlight actions and results.

5. Discuss the appraisal with the employee

This is generally the step in the process that is the most difficult for managers and employees alike and it can be a challenge to manage emotions and expectations. Even when performance is strong, there can be differences of opinion on the next action. A significant difference of opinion regarding performance can create an emotionally-charged situation. If the manager is providing feedback and coaching regularly, this shouldn't be the case. A related point: If an employee has consistently poor performance, the issue should be addressed—corrective action is taken—on time and not deferred to an annual review. To identify and prepare for differences of opinion, management can ask employees to complete and submit a self-evaluation before the appraisal meeting. A key point to keep in mind is that the manager's ability to remain calm and civil will have a significant impact on the employee's confidence, motivation, and future performance.

6. Implement personnel action

The final step in the appraisal process is the discussion and/or implementation of any next steps: a reward of some sort—a raise, promotion, or coveted development opportunity—or corrective action—a performance plan or termination. Note, however, that corrective action that might help an employee achieve expectations shouldn't be tabled until the next formal appraisal. As performance gaps are identified, supervisors and managers should take the time to identify why performance is not meeting expectations and determine whether the employee can meet expectations with additional training and/or coaching.

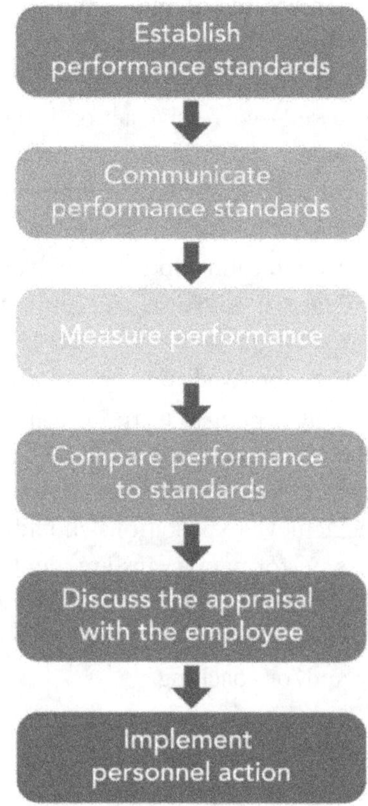

Requirements of a Sound Performance Appraisal Programme

A sound system of performance appraisal must fulfill the following essentials :

1. The appraisal plan should be simple to operate and easy to understand. When the appraisal system is complicated, employees may not understand it fully and may look at the plan with suspicion. The plan should not be very time-consuming.

2. The performance appraisal system should be performance-based uniform and non-variable fair, just, and equitable. It should be ensured

that the appraisers are honest. rational and objective in their approach to judgement and behavioural orientation.

3. The employees should be made aware of the performance goals targets, behaviour, etc expected of them A personal equation between the appraiser and the employee has to be developed to achieve a mutual understanding of the criteria of evaluation

4. The appraisal plan should be devised in consultation with subordinates. This will increase their commitment to the plan and their understanding of expected performance

5. The appraisal plan should take into account the appraisal practices prevailing in other units in the industry as well as the latest thinking on performance appraisal. It should fit into the structure and operations of the organisation

6. The top management must create a climate of reliable appraisal throughout the organisation. Goal orientation, open communications mutual trust informal relationships, etc are the basic elements of such a climate

7 The appraisal plan should be designed to achieve specific objectives. The objectives of the appraisal program may be to evaluate current performance on the job and to determine the potential for higher jobs. In some cases, performance appraisal is linked with specific objectives like pay raise, training, promotion, transfer, etc The number of factors to be considered and the data to be collected should be tailormade to achieve the objective of the appraisal

8. The appraisers should be selected and trained properly so that they have no personal bias and possess the necessary capabilities for the objective evaluation of employees. To ensure objectivity in the appraisal, an individual may independently be rated by more persons.

9. There should be a provision of appeals against appraisals to ensure the confidence of the employees and their associations or unions. The results of the appraisal must be discussed with the rates so that they may get an opportunity to express their feelings on their progress reports.

CHAPTER VIII

CAREER PLANNING

A career is a sequence of attitudes and behaviours associated with a series of job and work-related activities over a person's lifetime. It may be defined as a succession of related jobs, arranged in hierarchical order, through which a person moves in an organisation.

A career is often defined separately as an external career and an internal career. External career refers to the objective categories used by society and organisations to describe the progression of steps through a given occupation, while internal career refers to the set of steps or stages which make up the individual's concept of career progression within an occupation. For such two different approaches, in organisational context, a career can be identified as an integrated pace of vertical and lateral movement in an occupation of an individual over his employment span. Such an integrated approach is intended to minimize the diversity of hopes and expectations of employees matching individually perceived careers with organization-centered careers.

The term 'career denotes all the jobs that are held during one's working life. It is viewed as a sequence of positions held by an individual during his lifetime. Edwin B. Flippo defined a career as a sequence of separate but related work activities that provide continuity, order, and meaning in a person's life.

Career Anchors

Career anchors denote the basic drives that create the urge to take up a certain type of career. These drives are as follows:

- Managerial Competence: A person having this drive seeks managerial positions that provide opportunities for higher responsibility, decision making, control, and influence over others.
- Technical Competence: People having this anchor seek to make career choices based on the technical or functional content of the work. It provides continuous learning and updating one's expertise in a technical or specialised area such as quality control, engineering, accounting, advertising, public relations, etc.

- Security: If one's career anchor is security then he is willing to do what is required to maintain job security (through compliance with organisational prescriptions), a decent income, and a stable future.
- Creativity: This drive provides entrepreneurial and innovative opportunities to the people. People are driven by an overwhelming desire to do something new that is total of their own making.
- Autonomy: These people seek a career that provides freedom of action and independence.

Career planning

Career planning is an individual's lifelong process of establishing personal career objectives and acting in a manner intended to bring them about. It refers to the active management of your career and the structured planning of its future. To effectively plan your career, you should take into consideration your personality, your skillset, and your desired role alongside the changing needs of the job market. Career planning is an ongoing process through which an individual sets career goals and identifies the means to achieve them. The process by which individuals plan their life's work is referred to as career planning

When you plan your career, you decide on a path that will meet your needs (financial, emotional, or otherwise) and manifest your aspirations. It's all about making better decisions for yourself so that you can live the life you dream of. Career planning helps you make decisions throughout your career, whether you are just starting or planning retirement.

"Career planning is a process of systematically matching career goals and individual capabilities with opportunities for their fulfillment."(Schermerhorn: 2002)

"Career Planning is a deliberate process of becoming aware of self, opportunities, constraints, choices, and consequences; identifying career-related goals; and "career pathing" or programming work, education, and related developmental experiences to provide the direction, timing, and sequence of steps to attain a specific career goal." McMahon and Merman: 1987

Nature of Career Planning
The following are the salient features of career planning

- A Process: Career planning is a process of developing human resources rather than an event.
- Upward movement: It involves upward movement in the organisational hierarchy, or special assignments, project work that requires abilities to handle recurring problems, human relations issues, and so on.
- Mutuality of Interest: The individual's interest is served as his needs and aspirations are met to a great extent and the organisation's interest is served as each of its human resources is provided an opportunity to develop and contribute to the organisational goals and objectives to the optimum of its ability and confidence.
- Dynamic Career planning is dynamic due to an ever-changing environment.

Objectives of Career Planning

Career Planning seeks to meet the following objectives:

- To provide and maintain appropriate manpower resources in the organisation by offering careers, not jobs.
- To provide an environment for the effectiveness, efficiency, and growth of its employees and motivate them to contribute effectively towards achieving the objectives of the organisation.
- To map out careers of various categories of employees suitable to their ability, and their willingness to be 'trained and developed for higher positions.
- To have a stable workforce by reducing absenteeism and employee turnover.
- To cater to the immediate and future human resources need of the organisation on a timely basis.
- To increase the utilisation of managerial reserves within organisation.

Steps in Career Planning Process

1. Self-Assessment: The first and foremost step in career planning is to know and assess yourself. You need to collect information about yourself while deciding about a particular career option. You must analyse your interests, abilities, aptitudes, desired lifestyle, and personal traits and then study the relationship between the career opted for and self.

2. Goal Setting: Set your goals according to your academic qualification, work experience, priorities, and expectations in life. Once your goal is

identified, then you determine the feasible ways and objectives how to realize it.

3. Academic/Career Options: Narrow your general occupational direction to a particular one by an informatory decision-making process. Analyse the career option by keeping in mind your present educational qualification and what more academic degrees you need to acquire for it.

4. Plan of action: The plan of action recognizes those industries and particular companies that you want to get into. Make the plan a detailed one so that you can determine for how many years you are going to work in a company to achieve maximum success, and then switch to another. Decide where you would like to see yourself after five years and in which position.

5. Catch Hold of Opportunities: Opportunity comes but once. So, whenever you get any opportunity to prove yourself and get into your desired career, try to convert it in every way for suiting your purpose. Remember, a successful professional is also quite opportunistic in his moves, examining every opening to turn in his favour.

Follow these 4 steps to plan your individual career.

Step 1: Get to know yourself

Identify your vision, values, interests, skills, traits, and abilities. It will help you decide what you want from your next career move. Then, think about your answers to these questions:

- Choosing a new career direction: Which of your core values are most important to your choice?
- Looking for new challenges at work: Which of your skills or interests could help you develop and advance?
- Considering going back to school: Which type of program would make the most of your strengths?

Step 2: Explore your occupational options

Explore your options and gather information about them. What choices do you have? What does each one involve? Are there other options you haven't thought about?

- Choosing a career direction: Find out about the occupations that interest you. Try talking with people in those fields. Can you get direct experience by volunteering? What about working part-time or job-shadowing? Don't forget to consider related occupations.

- Considering going back to school: Talk to people in the occupations that interest you. Ask how they gained the skills and knowledge they needed. Get their advice on the training options that employers prefer.

Step 3: Make your decision by evaluating your career options

Evaluate your career options. Decide which ones are best for you at this stage of your life. Look at the pros and cons of each option. Consider the challenges you may face and how you can handle them.

Step 4: Take action to achieve your career goals

Develop a plan to make your options a reality. Identify the short-term and long-term steps that you need to take. Create deadlines for the completion of each step. Identify things you can do to stay motivated. Then take the steps you've identified.

Use career planning to take charge of the changes in your life and work. Career planning is a practical way to manage the ongoing changes in one's life and work. It helps you build on what you already have and think realistically about your priorities.

CHAPTER IX

COMPENSATION MANAGEMENT GRIEVANCE REDRESSAL

Compensation Management includes various areas such as job evaluation, surveys of wages and salary analysis of the relevant organisational problems, development of suitable wage structure, framing of rules for administering wages and salaries, wage payment, incentive, control of compensation cost, etc.

Compensation is defined as the consolidated amount, allowances received, and various other kinds of benefits and services which are offered by the organisation to their employees. In other words, compensation refers to all forms of financial returns, services, and benefits received by the employees from their organisation as a part of their employment relationship.

Such compensation may be received in the form of cash i.e. wages/salaries, bonus, overtime payments, or incentives (i.e. gross payment). This is called 'direct compensation. While benefits that come under indirect compensation may consist of life, accidents and health insurance, pay for vacation or illness, retirement benefits, and so on.

Thus, in short, compensation is direct and indirect monetary benefits and rewards received by employees based on the value of the jobs, their contributions, and overall performance. Such rewards are given to employees by their organisation according to the ability of the organisation to pay and the legal provisions.

Objectives of Compensation Management

1. To attract competent and qualified persons to an organization by offering fair wages and incentives.

2. To retain present employees by paying competitive remuneration.

3. To establish fair and equitable remuneration to avoid pay disparities.

4. To improve the production, productivity, and profitability of the organization.

5. To minimise unnecessary expenditure and to control cost through a device of internal check and establishment of a standard.

6. To improve and maintain good human relations between employer and employee through a process of payment of bonus, profit sharing, and other fringe benefits.

7. To enhance the name and fame of the company through a proper system of wage payment.

8. To ensure prompt and regular payment of wage and salary to all the employees.

<u>Components of Compensation</u>

Compensation is the reward or remuneration paid to the employees in return for the service rendered. Such compensation package includes both monetary and non-monetary components.

In India compensation or pay structure generally consists of the following components:

- Wage or Salary
- Dearness and other allowances
- Incentives
- Fringe benefits and perquisites.

1. Wage or Salary:

Wage:

The term wage refers to the remuneration paid to the workers appointed on an hourly, daily, or weekly basis in return for the service rendered. It varies according to the physical and mental requirements of the job. Wage may be minimum wage, fair wage, and a living wage.

i. Minimum Wage:

It is that wage that is sufficient to meet the basic need of a worker and his family. This minimum wage has to be paid to the worker irrespective of the capacity of the industry to pay. The Committee on fair wage has defined minimum wage as – "the wage must provide not only for the bare sustenance of life but for the preservation of the efficiency of the workers. For this purpose, minimum wage must provide some measures of education, medical requirements and amenities".

ii. Fair Wage:

According to the committee on fair wage "fair wage is the wage which is above the minimum wage but, below the living wage". It is fixed between the minimum wage and the capacity to pay by the industry. The lower limit of the fair wage is the minimum wage; the upper limit is set by the capacity of the industry to pay.

Fair wage depends on several factors like:

(a) The productivity of labour

(b) The prevailing rates of wage in the same or neighboring localities.

(c) The level of national income and its distribution.

(d) The place of industry in the economy of the country.

Thus, a fair wage is determined based on capacity of the industry to pay and the region in which the industry is located.

iii. Living Wage:

It is the wage that provides some of the comforts of life. It provides certain amenities considered necessary for the well-being of the worker. According to the Fair Wage Committee "the living wage should enable the male earner to provide for himself and his family not merely the bare essentials of food, clothing, and shelter but also a measure of frugal (using only as much money or food as is necessary) comfort including education for children, protection against ill health, requirements of essential social needs and measure of insurance against the more important misfortunes including old age".

Salary:

The term salary refers to remuneration paid to the employees appointed on a monthly or annual basis in return for the service rendered. Thus it refers to the monthly rate of pay irrespective of the number of hours put in by employees.

Take Home Salary:

It is the net amount of salary received by an employee after making all the deductions towards the payment of income tax, LIC premium, and contribution to P.F., etc.

2. Dearness Allowance (DA):

Under section 3 of the Minimum Wages Act, DA is described as a cost of living allowance. It is given to protect the real wages of workers during inflation. In India, it has become an integral part of the wage system.

Along with DA other allowances like City Compensatory Allowance (CCA), House Rent Allowance (HRA), Medical Allowance (MA), Education Allowance (EA), Conveyance Allowance, etc., also form the part of the compensation package.

However, the inclusion of all these allowances in the compensation depends on the nature and type of job, contents of job, place of job, terms, and condition of appointment, the capacity of the employer, etc.

3. Incentives:

An incentive is a reward paid in addition to wages whether monetary or not that motivates or compensates an employee for performance above the standard. Payment of incentives depends on the productivity, sales, and Profit of the organization.

4. Fringe Benefits and Perquisites:

Fringe Benefits:

It is a general term used to describe any of a variety of non-wage or supplemental benefits that employees receive in addition to their regular wages. These include such employee benefits as provident fund, gratuity, medical care, hospitalization, accident relief, paid holidays, health and group insurance, pension, etc.

Perquisites (Perks):

Perquisites also called perks are the special benefits made available only to the top executives of an organisation. These may include a company car, furnished house, stock option scheme, club membership, paid holidays etc.

Major Factors Influencing Compensation

The factors affecting employee compensation can be categorized into:-

1. Internal Factors and 2. External Factors.

I. External Determinants of Compensation:

1. Labour Market Conditions:

The forces of demand and supply of human resources, no doubt, play a role in compensation decision. Employees with rare skill sets and expertise gained through experience command higher wage and salary than the ones with ordinary skills abundantly available in the job market. But the higher supply of human resources for certain jobs may not lead to reduction of wages beyond a floor level due to the Government's prescription of minimum wage levels and employee union's bargaining strength.

Similarly, this factor by itself does not result in lower pay if the vast majority of available resources are unemployable due to poor skill and low talent. Thus, it is clear that law of demand and supply applies to labour market only to a limited extent.

2. Economic Conditions:

Organizations having state-of-the-art technology in place, excellent productivity records, higher operational efficiency, a pool of skilled manpower, etc., can be better pay masters. Thus, compensation is the consequence of the level of competitiveness .prevailing in a given industry.

3. Prevailing Wage Level:

Most of the organizations fix their pay in keeping with the level for similar jobs in the industry. They frequently conduct wage survey and accordingly seek to keep their wage level for different jobs. If a particular firm keeps its pay level higher than those of others in the industry, its employee cost becomes heavier which may escalate the end cost of the products. This will affect the competitiveness of the firm. On the other hand, if a firm keeps its pay level lower than the prevailing rates, it may not recruit the skilled and competent manpower.

4. Government Control:

Government through various legislative enactments such as Minimum Wages Act, 1948, Payment of Wage Act, 1936, Equal Remuneration Act, 1976, Payment of Bonus Act, 1965, dealing with Provident Funds, Gratuity, Companies Act, etc., have a bearing on compensation decisions. Therefore, firms have to decide on salaries and wages in the light of the relevant Acts.

5. Cost of Living:

Increase in the cost of living, raise the cost of goods and services. It varies from area to area within a country and from country to country. The changes in compensation are based on consumer price index which measures the average change in the price of basic necessities like food, clothing, fuel, medical service, etc., over a period of time. Allowances like Dearness Allowance. City compensatory allowances are paid to meet the increasing cost of living and parity among employees posted at different geographies.

6. Union's Influence:

The collective bargaining strength of the trade unions also influence the wage levels. Trade unions enjoy an upper hand in certain industries like banking, insurance, transport and other public utilities. Therefore, wage structure in such industries and in such Union-active regions, salary and wage need to be fixed and revised in consultation with the unions for ensuring smooth industrial relation.

7. Globalization:

It has ushered in an era of higher compensation level in many sectors of the economy. The entry of multinational corporations and big corporates have triggered a massive change in the compensation structure of companies across sectors. There is a salary boom in sectors like information technology, hospitality, biotechnology, electronics, financial services and so on.

8. Cross Sector Mobility:

Contemporary companies find it difficult to benchmark the salaries of their staff with others in the industry thanks to mobility of talent across the sectors. For example, hospitality sector employees are hired by airlines, BPOs, healthcare companies and telecom companies.

II. Internal Determinants of Compensation:

1. Compensation Policy of the Organization:

Firm's policy regarding pay i.e., attitude to be an industry leader in pay or desire to pay the market rate determines its pay structure. The former can attract better talent and achieve lower cost per unit of labour than the ones that pay competitive pay.

2. Employer's Affordability:

Those organizations which earn high profit and have a larger market share, a large business conglomerate and multinational companies can afford to pay higher pay than others. Besides, company's ability to pay higher pay is impaired by sector- specific economic recession and acute competition.

3. Worth of a Job:

Organizations base their pay level on the worth of a job. The wages and salaries tend to be higher for jobs involving exercise of brain power, responsibility laden jobs, creativity-oriented jobs, technical jobs.

4. Employee's Worth:

In some organizations, time rates are granted to all employees irrespective of performance. In such cases, employees are rewarded for their mere physical presence on the job rather than for their performance. However many private sector organizations follow performance-linked pay system. They conduct performance appraisal more often than not which provides input for determining pay levels. It distinguishes the high-performer from the low-performer and the non-performer.

The amount of compensation received by an employee should take into account several factors such as the amount of effort put in, competitive rates prevailing in labour market, demand for and supply of labour, the firm's ability to pay, labour policy, etc.

1. The Organisation's Ability to Pay:

Wage increases should be given by those organisations which can afford them. Companies that have good sales and, therefore, high profits tend to pay higher wages than those which running at a loss or earning low profits because of the high cost of production or low sales. In the short run, the economic influence on the ability to pay is practically nil. All employers, irrespective of their profits or losses, must pay no less than their competitors and need pay no more if they wish to attract and keep workers.

In the long run, the ability to pay is very important. During the time of prosperity, employers pay high wages to carry on profitable operations and because of their increased ability to pay. But during a period of depression, wages are cut because funds are not available. Marginal firms and non-profit organisations (like hospitals and educational institutions) pay relatively low wages because of low or no profits.

2. Supply of and Demand for Labour:

The labour market conditions or supply and demand forces operate at the national, regional and local levels, and determine organisational wage structure and level.

If the demand for certain skills is high and the supply is low, the result is a rise in the price to be paid for these skills. When prolonged and acute, these labour-market pressures probably force most organisations to "reclassify hard-to-fill jobs at a higher level" than that suggested by the job evaluation. The other alternative is to pay higher wages if the labour supply is scarce; and lower wages when it is excessive.

Similarly, if there is great demand for labour expertise, wages rise; but if the demand for manpower skill is minimal, the wages will be relatively low. Mescon says- "The supply and demand compensation criterion is very closely related to the prevailing pay, comparable wage and ongoing wage concepts since, in essence, all of these remuneration standards are determined by immediate market forces and factors."

3. Prevailing Market Rate:

This is also known as the 'comparable wage' or 'going wage rate', and is the most widely used criterion. An organisation's compensation policies generally tend to conform to the wage rates payable by the industry and the community. This is done for several reasons. First, competition demands that competitors adhere to the same relative wage level. Second, various government laws and judicial decisions make the adoption of uniform wage rates an attractive proposition.

Third, trade unions encourage this practice so that their members can have equal pay, equal work and geographical differences may be eliminated. Fourth, functionally related firms in the same industry require essentially the same quality of employees, with the same skills and experience. This results in a considerable uniformity in wage and salary rates.

Finally, if the same or about the same general rates of wages are not paid to the employees as are paid by the organisation's competitors, it will not be able to attract and maintain a sufficient quantity and quality of manpower. Belcher and Atchison observe- "Some companies pay on the high side of the market in order to obtain goodwill or to insure an adequate supply of labour, while other organisations pay lower wages because economically they have to, or because by lowering hiring requirements they can keep jobs adequately manned."

4. The Cost of Living:

The cost of living pay criterion is usually regarded as an automatic minimum equity pay criterion. This criterion calls for pay adjustments based on increases or decreases in an acceptable cost of living index. In recognition of the influence of the cost of
living, "escalator clauses" are written into labour contracts.

When the cost of living increases, workers and trade unions demand adjusted wages to offset the erosion of real wages. However, when living costs are stable or decline, the management does not resort to this argument as a reason for wage reductions.

5. The Living Wage:

The living wage criterion means that wages paid should be adequate to enable an employee to maintain himself and his family at a reasonable level of existence. However, employers do not generally favour using the concept of a living wage as a guide to wage determination because they prefer to base the wages of an employee on his contribution rather than on his need. Also, they feel that the level of living prescribed in a worker's budget is open to argument since it is based on subjective opinion.

6. Productivity:

Productivity is another criterion, and is measured in terms of output per man-hour. It is not due to labour efforts alone. Technological improvements, better organisation and management, the development of better methods of production by labour and management, greater ingenuity and skill by labour are all responsible for the increase in productivity. Actually, productivity measures the contribution of all the resource factors — men, machines, methods, materials, and management.

No productivity index can be devised which will measure only the productivity of a specific factor of production. Another problem is that productivity can be measured at several levels — job, plant, industry or national, or economic level. Thus, although theoretically, it is a sound compensation criterion, operationally many problems and complications arise because of definitional measurement and conceptual issues.

7. Trade Union's Bargaining Power:

Trade unions do affect the rate of wages. Generally, the stronger the trade union, the higher the wages. A trade union's bargaining power is often measured in terms of its membership, its financial strength, and the nature of its leadership. A strike or a threat of a strike is the most powerful weapon used by it.

Sometimes trade unions force wages up faster than productivity increases would allow and become responsible for unemployment or higher prices and inflation. However, for those remaining on the payroll, a real gain is often achieved as a consequence of a trade union's stronger bargaining power.

8. Job Requirements:

Generally, the more difficult a job, the higher the wages. Measures of job difficulty are frequently used when the relative value of one job to another in an organisation is to be ascertained. Jobs are graded according to the relative skill, effort, responsibility, and job conditions required.

9. Managerial Attitudes:

These have a decisive influence on the wage structure and wage level since judgment is exercised in many areas of wage and salary administration — including whether the firm should pay below average, or above average rates, what job factors should be used to reflect job worth, the weight to be given for performance or length of service, and so forth, both the structure and level of wages are bound to be affected accordingly. These matters require the approval of the top executives.

Lester observes "Top management's desire to maintain or enhance the company's prestige has been a major factor in the wage policy of several firms. Desires to improve or maintain morale, to attract high-caliber employees, to reduce turnover, and to provide a high living standard for employees as possible also appear to be factored in management's wage policy decisions."

10. Psychological and Social Factors:

These determine in a significant measure how hard a person will work for the compensation received or what pressures he will exert to get his compensation increased. Psychologically, people perceive the level of wages as a measure of success in life; people may feel secure; have an inferiority complex, seem inadequate or feel the reverse of this. They may not take pride in their work, or in the wages they get.

Therefore, these things should not be overlooked by the management in establishing wage rates. Sociologically and ethically, people feel that "equal work should carry equal wages," that "wages should be commensurate with their efforts," that "they are not exploited, and that no distinction is made based on caste, colour, sex, or religion."

To satisfy the conditions of equity, fairness, and justice, management should consider these factors.

11. Skill Levels Available in the Market:

With the rapid growth of industries, businesses, and trade, there is a shortage of skilled resources. Technological development and automation have been affecting the skill levels at faster rates. Thus, the wage levels of skilled employees are constantly changing and an organisation has to keep its level up to suit the market needs.

CHAPTER X

GRIEVANCE REDRESSAL

Grievance refers to the employee's dissatisfaction with the company's work policy and conditions because of an alleged violation of the law. They may or may not be justified and usually represent the gap between what the employee expects and gets from the company. Employees can have grievances with each other, with their managers, or even with clients. A grievance is a sign of an employee's discontent with the job and its nature. The employee has got certain aspirations and expectations that he thinks must be fulfilled by the organisation where he is working. When the organisation fails to satisfy the employee's needs, he develops a feeling of discontent or dissatisfaction. A grievance redressal mechanism is important for tracking the number and frequency of grievances which signify the efficiency of an organisation. Grievance has to be properly addressed because it lowers the motivation and performance of the employee and affects the work environment.

A well-defined grievance procedure is a vital element of a good industrial relations machinery. Prompt and effective disposal of workers' grievances is the key to industrial peace. The grievance procedure set up by agreement with a union provides a medium for the workers to transmit their grievance to management in an orderly manner and get the answer in writing.

According to Michael J. Jucius, the term 'grievance' means "any discontent or dissatisfaction, whether expressed or not and whether valid or not, arising out of anything connected with the company that an employee thinks, believes or even feels, is unfair, just, or inequitable."

In the words of Edward Flippo, "It is a type of discontent which must always be expressed. A grievance is usually more formal in character than a complaint. It can be valid or ridiculous and must grow out of something connected with company operations or policy. It must involve an interpretation or application of the provisions of the labour contract".

Keith Davis has defined grievance as "any real or imagined feeling of personal injustice which an employee has concerning his employment relationship." A grievance represents a situation in which an employee feels that something unfavourable to him has happened or is going to happen. In an industrial enterprise, a grievance may arise because of several factors such as:

(a) violation of management's responsibility such as poor working conditions,

(b) violation of the company's rules and practices.

(c) violation of collective bargaining agreement,

(d) violation of labour laws,

(e) violation of natural rules of justice such as unfair treatment in the promotion.

Sources of Grievances

The causes of grievances may be grouped under three heads, viz., (1) management policies; (ii) working conditions; (ii) personal factors.

(i) Grievances resulting from Management Policies

(a) Wage rates or scale of pay

(b) Overtime

(c) Leave

(d) Transfer-improper matching of the worker with the job

(e) Seniority, promotion, and discharges

(f)Lack of career planning and employee development plan

(g) Lack of role clarity

(h) Lack of regard for a collective agreement

(i) Hostility towards a labour union:

(j)Autocratic leadership style of supervisors

(ii) Grievances resulting from Working Conditions:

(a) Unrealistic working conditions

(b) Non-availability of proper tools, machines, and equipment for doing the job

(c) Tight production standards

(d) Adverse physical conditions of the workplace

(e) Poor relationship with the supervisor

(f)Negative approach to discipline

(iii) Grievances resulting from Personal Factors:

(a) Narrow attitude

(b) Over-ambition

(c) Egoistic personality.

Ways to discover Employee Grievances

The grievances redressal procedure gives an assurance to the employees about the existence of a mechanism for the prompt redressal of their grievance. There are a few grievance identification techniques like open door policy, exit interviews, opinion surveys, and gripe boxes. The best approach toward grievances is to anticipate them and take steps to tackle them before they grievances assume dangerous proportions. An ordinary manager redresses grievances as and when they arise. An excellent manager anticipates and prevents them.

Managers can know and understand grievances with the help of the following methods:

1. Exit Interview: An interview of every employee who quits the organisation can reveal employee grievances. Most of the employees quit the company due to some dissatisfaction. A great amount of care and empathy is necessary for a successful exit interview.

2. Opinion Surveys. A survey may be conducted to elicit the opinions of employees regarding the organisation and its management Group meetings periodical interviews with workers and collective bargaining sessions are also helpful in knowing employee discontent before it becomes a grievance

3. Gripe Boxes: These are boxes in which the employees can drop their anonymous complaints in the organisations about the causes of dissatisfaction. It is different from the suggestion scheme system in which employees drop their named suggestions with the intention to receive rewards.

4. Open Door Policy: Under this procedure, the employees are free to meet the top executive of the organisation and get their grievances redressed. Such a policy may work well in small organisations, but in big organisations this may not be practicable because the top executive will be too busy with other matters Another disadvantage of an open-door policy is that lower-level executives feel bypassed This may complicate the human relations problems Moreover top management is not too familiar with the working conditions of the operative employees It may be difficult for it to attend to employee grievances because of lack of sufficient information. Lastly, it is also said that the open-door policy is suitable for executives to walk through and not the operative employees. The employees may even hesitate to go to top executives with their grievances

Different types of grievances

1. Visible Grievances or Hidden Grievances: When the grievances are clearly visible to others are called visible grievances. But it is not necessary that all times these are visible then these are called hidden one. It is called hidden grievances.

2. Real or Imaginary: The grievances may be real or imaginary also. These may be called genuine or imaginary too. When a grievance is due to a valid reason and related to the terms of employment only. The management or concerned party responsible for redressing grievance is called real, genuine, or factual grievance. Second, the imaginary grievance is that when it is there not for any valid reason. The management is not at fault. It is called imaginary only.

3. Expressed or Implied: There may be expressed or implied grievances. When an employee felt a grievance and expressed or reports to the management in written or oral forms, is called express because it has been made clear. When it is not made clear but from the situation, it can be inferred or judged that there is a grievance. That type of grievance is called an implied grievance.

4. Oral or Written: According to the way of expression, the grievances can be oral or written. When orally it is reported or expressed then it is called an oral grievance. An employee makes a written complaint then it becomes a written grievance. Entirely according to their expression the grievances are classified.

5. Disguised Grievances: Sometimes the grievances take place but the employees do not know the reasons for grievances. The causes of grievances are unknown. These are called disguised grievances. This type of grievance occurs due to mental pressure or frustration due to other factors and is unrelated to work.

6. Individual or Group Grievances: The grievances may be related to an individual employee or a group of employees. In a group, we may include a team, department, etc. When an individual is affected then it is called an individual grievance. When a group is affected due to the grievances and reported then it becomes a group grievance. Other factors for forming types are not considered other than the party affected.

7. Union Grievances: The union presents the grievances to the management on behalf of member employees then it becomes a union

grievance. It is presented in the interest of everyone in the union and not for an individual employee. When the employees felt that the terms of employment are violated then the union takes the initiative in reporting the grievances. The union presents the case for collective agreements in this case.

8. Policy Grievances: When a grievance is related to the policy of the company relating to terms of employment is called a policy grievance. The terms of employment may include appointment, training, compensation, promotion and transfer, rewards and incentives, bonus, allowances, etc. When these are violated by the management and reported by the employees' union then it becomes a policy grievance.

Essentials of a Sound Grievance Procedure

An effective grievance procedure should contain the following characteristics

1. Legal Sanctity. The procedure should be in conformity with the existing law it should be designed to supplement the statutory provisions Wherever possible the procedure should make use of the machinery provided under legislation The procedure may be incorporated in the standing orders or collective bargaining agreement of the organisation

2. Acceptability. The grievance procedure must be acceptable to all and should therefore be developed with mutual consultation among management workers and the union. In order to be generally accepted the procedure must ensure

(a) a sense of fair play and justice to workers

(b) reasonable exercise of authority to managers, and

(c) reasonable participation in the union

3. Promptness. The grievance procedure must aim at speedy redressal of grievances This can be ensured in the following ways

(a) as far as possible the grievance should be settled at the lowest level.

(b) there should be only one appeal

(c) time limits should be prescribed and rigidly enforced at each level and

(d) different types of grievances may be referred to appropriate authorities

4. Simplicity. The procedure should consist of as few steps as possible Channels for handling grievances should be carefully developed Employees must know the officers to be contacted at each level Information about the procedure should be communicated to the employees.

5. Training. Supervisors and union representatives should be given training in grievance handling. This will help to ensure effective working of the grievance procedure.

6. Follow-up. The working of the grievance procedure should be reviewed at periodical intervals. Necessary improvements should be made to make the procedure more effective.

Grievance handling Procedure

Grievance handling is the management and redressal of grievances by the HR department. It is one of the responsibilities of the department to set up a formal process to redress employee grievances. Model grievance Procedure in India provides five successive time-bound steps each leading to the next in case the aggrieved employee prefers an appeal. These steps are as follows:

(i) An aggrieved employee shall first present his grievance verbally in person to the officer nominated/ appointed by the management for this purpose The officer must give his answer within forty-eight hours of the presentation of the complaint

(ii) If the employee does not receive an answer within the stipulated time or he is not satisfied with the answer he shall either in person or with his departmental (or any representative) present his grievance to the head of the department designated for this purpose The departmental head is required to furnish his answer within three days of the presentation of the grievance.

(iii)If the employee is not satisfied with the answer, he can approach the Grievance Committee which shall evaluate the case and make its recommendations to management within seven days of presentation of the case The employee would be communicated the recommendation within three days

(iv) If the committee fails to take a decision within the stipulated period or the employee is not satisfied with the decision he can make an appeal for revision to management Management is supposed to communicate its decision within seven days of the worker's revised petition

(e) If the employee is unsatisfied with the management's decision. union and management may refer to grievance to voluntary arbitration within a week of the receipt of management's decision by the aggrieved employee.

How do you write a grievance description?

A grievance description or a grievance letter must have the following attributes:

- The letter must clearly state the type of grievance and then the actual grievance.
- It must be to the point and must get to the issue directly
- It should state the facts, as objectively as possible
- It would be advisable to not use any offensive language or obscenities
- The letter is not about expressing anger but should objectively mention what the employee is feeling and what is the reason it has become a grievance for the employee
- It should conclude by asking for swift redressal and willingness to cooperate with the concerned people for the same

How to deal with grievances at work?

Disconcerted employees can pull down the productivity of an organisation. Hence, it is important for HRs to build a system of hearing and redressing employee grievances. It can be done through the following simple steps:

1. Create a mechanism: HRs can use a well-designed HRMS to build a strong system of gathering and processing employee grievances.
2. Listen more than talk: While hearing the grievances, it is a good idea to practice deep listening and empathize with the griever to fully understand what they are unhappy about.
3. Inquire and investigate: Once you have the employees' point of view on the matter, set in motion your own inquiry to understand all the facets of the issue and figure out the root cause.
4. Hold a formal meeting: Call in all the relevant parties and ask the employee to present any evidence to back up their issue. You can also ask them about how they would like the issue to be resolved
5. Decide and act: Once you reach a conclusion, make a decision you think is best and then act on the resolution.

6. Set up and communicate the appeal process: Have a system in place that allows the employee to formally appeal in case they are unhappy with the resolution. Clearly communicate the rules for the same.
7. Review the situation: Decide on a relevant time interval and review the situation to understand if any further intervention is required. Act accordingly.
8. Analyse and plan ahead: Retrospect and gather insights about different issues and plan to prevent the same problems in the future.

Points to be Kept in Mind while Handling a Grievance

The following points are relevant to be kept in mind during handling a grievance:

1. Every grievance must be given due respect and considered important.

2. A grievance should not be postponed with the hope that people will "see the light" themselves.

3. A grievance should be put in writing.

4. Relevant facts about a grievance should be gathered by management and their proper records should be maintained.

5. The employee should be given free time off to pursue his grievance.

6. Management should take a list of all solutions and later evaluate them one by one in terms of their total effect on the organisation.

7. Decision once reached should be communicated to the employee and acted upon by the management.

8. Follow-up must be done by the management to determine whether the action taken by it has favourably changed the employee's attitude or not.